Aurea Vidyā Collection*

— 18 —

* For a complete list of titles, see page 213.

Published by Aurea Vidyā
39 West 88th Street, New York, N.Y. 10024
www.vidya-ashramvidyaorder.org

This book was originally published in Italian as
Śaṅkara, *Aparokṣānubhūti*, Autorealizzazione, by
Edizioni Āśram Vidyā, Rome, Italy 1975

First published in English in 2015 as
Śaṅkara, *Aparokṣānubhūti*, Self-Realization, by
Aurea Vidyā, New York, N.Y. 10024

Printed and bound by Lightning Source Inc. at locations in the U.S.A. and abroad, as shown on the last page.

ISBN: 978-1-931406-23-9
Library of Congress Control Number: 2014957081

Front cover: The "Green Lion."

Śaṅkara

Aparokṣānubhūti

Self-Realization

by

Raphael

(Āśram Vidyā Order)

AUREA VIDYĀ

TABLE OF CONTENTS

Notes to the Text 9

Preface 17

Alchemical *Opus* 21

Aparokṣānubhūti 23

Appendix: Knowledge and Ritual Action 109

Note to the Appendix 159

Sanskrit Text (Appendix) 163

Glossary 179

Raphael: Unity of Tradition 207

NOTES TO THE TEXT

The English Text

1. Square brackets [ ] are ours. They enclose terms and phrases that are understood in the text, as well as supplementary material that is considered helpful for a better understanding of the work.

2. Round brackets ( ) enclose the original Sanskrit of words and phrases that are under examination and that belong to the *sūtras* of the *Aparokṣānubhūti* and to the Śaṅkara "Introduction" to the *Śvetāśvatara Upaniṣad* (Appendix).

3. Double inverted commas " " enclose quotations from particular scriptural sources, while single inverted commas ' ' indicate speech within quotations.

4. Roman type is used for Sanskrit words (Brahman, Ātman, Hiraṇyagarbha, māya, etc.) in the *sūtras*, which otherwise appear in italic type. This pattern is reversed in the commentary.

5. The same noun will have an upper-case initial if it refers to a divine Form (*Vāyu*) and a lower-case initial if it refers to an element or form (*vāyu*).

6. Any discrepancies relating to scriptural references arise from the lack of uniformity in different editions and the different ways of dividing the texts from which they have been drawn.

The Sanskrit Text

1. The transliteration of the Sanskrit text from the original *devanāgarī* follows the currently accepted criteria and, apart from a few exceptions, does not separate the words.

2. References to verses in the *Upaniṣads* and other texts are given in accordance with the traditional numbering system used in the texts, such as *Muṇḍaka Upaniṣad* II.II.8-9.

The Phonetic Formation of the Letters

According to their mouthpositions

		gutturals	palatals	cerebrals	dentals	labials	
Simple breathing (formless sound)	h						
Release of breath	ḥ						
Vowels							
short		a	i	ṛ	ḷ	u	
long		ā	ī	ṝ	ḹ	ū	
		(a)					
Diphtongs			e-ai		o-au		
			(i)			(u)	
Semi-vowels			y	r	l	v	
Consonants							
unvoiced		k	c	ṭ	t	p	
aspirated unvoiced		kh	ch	ṭh	th	ph	
voiced		g	j	ḍ	d	b	
aspirated voiced		gh	jh	ḍh	dh	bh	
nasals		ṅ	ñ	ṇ	n	m	
Sibilants			ś	ṣ	s		
Pure nasal sound							ṁ
Nasal sound conformable to the consonant							ṃ

Guide to Pronunciation.

a = s**u**n
ā = f**a**ther
i = **i**f
ī = f**ee**t
u = p**u**t
ū = m**oo**n
ṛ = **ri**ng
ḷ = reve**lry**
e = **a**che
ai = m**i**ne
o = h**o**me
au = l**ou**d
k = **k**ite
kh = bloc**kh**ead
g = **g**ate
gh = lo**g-h**ut
ṅ = si**ng**
c = **ch**alk
ch = coa**ch-h**ouse
j = **j**ug
jh = he**dgeh**og
ñ = fri**n**ge
ṭ = dar**t***
ṭh = car**th**orse*
ḍ = or**d**er*
ḍh = har**d-h**eaded*
ṇ = cor**n***
t = **t**able
th = an**t-h**ill
d = **d**ay
dh = go**d-h**ead
n = **n**o
p = **p**ure
ph = loo**p-h**ole
b = **b**aby
bh = a**bh**or
m = **m**other
y = **y**ellow
r = **r**ed
l = **l**ady
v = **w**in
ś = **sh**all
ṣ = mar**sh***
s = **s**at
h = **he**aven
ṁ = b**onbon**
ḥ = aa**h**

* With the tip of the tongue raised to the roof of the mouth.

The knot of the heart is severed, all doubts dissipate, and for him [the effects of all] acts are destroyed when That, supreme and non-supreme, has been realized.

In the involucrum aureum sublime is Brahman, *without impurity and devoid of parts: That is perfectly clear, it is the light of the light. That is what the knower of the* ātman *realizes.*

Muṇḍaka Upaniṣad II.II.8-9

PREFACE

This short opus belongs to the series of works and specific treatises in prose and verse (*prakaraṇa*) that constitute the introductory basis to a deeper knowledge of the Initiatory Doctrine. Besides, it highlights particular aspects of it, and, in our case, the emphasis is placed on Realization. The result is a synthetic description of some principles of *Vedānta* and the exposition of fifteen means or steps through which Knowledge-realization can be attained.

Aparokṣānubhūti essentially deals with the identity of the *jīvātman* with *Brahman*, or unqualified Absolute, which is arrived at by removing the *avidyā* (metaphysical ignorance) through *vicāra* (discerning research).

For *Vedānta*, what binds the individual and fetters him to the world of *saṁsāra* is *avidyā*, which can be eliminated only through incisive discrimination-discernment and an investigation of real and non-real, of noumenon and phenomenon. *Avidyā*, *vicāra*, *vidyā*, *prārabdhakarma*, *jīvātman*, *Brahman* are fundamental terms of the *Vedānta* doctrine and are appropriately highlighted in the text.

Therefore, this brief treatise of metaphysical realization constitutes a valuable aid for those who want to travel the "Path of Fire," the "Path of *Advaita Vedānta*," the "Path of Being" supreme in its metaphysical aspect, the "Path of no contact" (*Asparśavāda*) of the "One-without-a-second." *Vedānta*, with the *mahāvākya* "That thou art" (*Tat tvam asi*) offers the highest realization a philosophical mind can conceive; it coincides with the unveiling of the Identity of nature of *jīva* and *ātman*, giving the *ens* the most secure beatitude and the *summa pax*.

The individual is in a multiplicity of conflicts because he has created a scissure, has obscured his true principial essence, has veiled the paradise dwelling in his soul.[1] There are no external objects, events or possessions, of any order or degree, that can reveal to him the peace he left behind in that moment in which, because of an act of free will, he went away from his own Source, ending up being dominated by his own *guṇas* and forcing himself into isolation.

One who truly wants to look for serenity and the joy without object must simply find himself again, understand his deepest nature and ardently realize it. All this implies not "abandoning" the world, "refusing" life or "opposing oneself" to the realm of perishable things, but merely comprehending what one is by resolving what one is not; this implies seeing the phenomenal world with the eye of *Vision* and recognizing the inescapable decline of the captivating and imprisoning *object*.

---

[1] For further information on the "scissure," see the chapter "The Fall of the Soul," in Raphael, *The Pathway of Non-Duality: Advaitavāda* (New York: Aurea Vidyā 2016).

Death and life, *avidyā* and liberation, pleasure and pain, love and hate, power and slavery can be *observed*, comprehended and won. But victory belongs to the daring and to those who are able to give a rhythm to their own life.

Aparokṣānubhūti unveils the means for the integral and final emancipation.

Concerning the author, Śaṅkara, introductions are not necessary; for Westerners, it needs only be said that he has been one of the most significant *yogi*-philosophers, if we can express it in this way, that India ever had. He has been the codifier of *Advaita Vedānta* (Non-duality), the metaphysical doctrine of the *Vedas-Upaniṣads*, and the most brilliant, fertile and profound commentator on many texts of the Indian tradition: from the *Brahmasūtra* to the *Bhagavadgītā*, to the major *Upaniṣads*, and so on.

R.

Aparokṣānubhūti - *Alchemical Opus*

The process of extraction of the *materia prima* from the form-name, realized in the final phase of alchemical *Opus*, "transmutation" or "transubstantiation," through a continuous process of *sublimation*, *distillation* and *fixation* of our true Nature, is synthesized in 15 steps in Śaṅkara's *Aparokṣānubhūti*.

The image of the Lion or Green Leo that swallows the Sun, presented on the cover of this book, is a complex symbol that expresses the whole alchemy of *Advaita*, the Sun that continuously emanates the Influx of the philosophical Mercury. It is *Tiphereth*, the Universal *Puruṣa*, the Healer-physician, the rectifier of metaphysical ignorance, the bearer of the real medicine (V.I.T.R.I.O.L.V.M.). Through him, the seals are purified and opened, expanded and exalted in the spiritual Heart of the researcher; here is the Law protected and secured in Love, alchemical Cross establishing in the manifestation the "right measure."

Using philosophical Mercury, Śaṅkara fixes only one *mantra* ("*Brahman* is everything and I am That") in the contemplative heart of the *jīva*. Exalted and offered to the intuition and penetration of the disciple throughout *Aparokṣānubhūti*, the *mantra*, as the light of the Green Lion, sublimates, distills and fixes.

Similarly, the Lion that swallows the Sun, like a *mantra*, is one and all at the same time...antimony, "guardian of the threshold," acid purifier that revitalizes, rectifying the *materia prima* after dessolving its saline clots. It is Water that does not wet, Fire that does not burn. It is the philosophical Mercury that swallows and, at the same time, is absorbed by the spiritual Sun-Leo in a sulphurous Dignity, symbol of the Divine hermaphrodite. It is not just male and female, but the polarity itself reintegrated at the center of the Garden of Eden, exalted in the Celestial Jerusalem, the *Sanāthanadharma* unveiled. In this context, the alchemical *Opus* expounded by Śaṅkara represents the right meditative "measure" to place in our Fire: *blazing*, "*Brahman* is everything" (here the *vāsanās* burn); *resolving*, "I am That" (here is the Silence, the sacrum itself, which has become neutral). The Lion swallows the Sun; all the qualities expressed are absorbed, dissolved, adjusted, fixed, internalized in pure Light. Thus, throughout this Work, Śaṅkara lets the purifying Influx of Consciousness ebb and flow in us.

Aurea Vidyā

Aparokṣānubhūti

śrī hariṁ paramānandam upadeṣṭāram īśvaram ।
vyāpakaṁ sarvalokānāṁ kāraṇaṁ taṁ namāmyaham ॥ 1 ॥

1. *I bow to* Śrī Hari [*Lord*], *supreme beatitude, first Master, all-pervasive and first cause of all the worlds.*

The *jīvātman* (the incarnate soul), apparently bound in slavery and error, bows, as first act, to the primordial *Hari* or *Īśvara*, the great Architect of the universe or *saguṇa Brahman*.

aparokṣānubhūtir vai procyate mokṣasiddhaye ।
sadbhir eva prayatnena vīkṣaṇīyā muhurmuhuḥ ॥ 2 ॥

2. *Here are explained in detail the means to obtain* aparokṣānubhūti [*realization of the* ātman] *and achieve integral liberation. One pure of heart, with persistence and yearning, will meditate on the truth here propounded.*

Aparokṣānubhūti is the direct perception or self-knowledge and, by extension, the very action or practice actualized in order to realize oneself as *ātman*. The ultimate aim of the individual is the comprehension of himself as integrated unity. If in time and space the individual can express indefinite existential qualifications toward his maturity, he cannot but place in front of himself the instance of self-recognition. Realization constitutes the gradual awakening of what we are in essence. This realization requires liberation from the qualities-attributes of phenomenal existence that veil our own essence and then emancipation from our dream life, the overcoming of all hurdles and of all fragmentations. Therefore, the problem of integral liberation can be posed by one who has reached *maturity*, the synthesis.

svavarṇāśramadharmeṇa tapasā haritoṣaṇāt |
sādhanaṁ prabhavet puṁsāṁ vairāgyādicatuṣṭayam || 3 ||

3. *The four means [preliminary for knowledge] as* vairāgya, *etc., are acquired by disciples through the practice of austerity, through the duties inherent in one's own stage of life and through the social order: this renders* Hari *propitious.*

In the *Vivekacūḍāmaṇi* of Śaṅkara we read:

"The Sages have said that for realization one must practice four qualifications, without which the attainment of *Brahman* could fail.

"The first one is discernment between the real and the non-real (*nityānityavastuvivekaḥ*); the second is detachment from the fruit of all actions in both this world and other worlds; the third consists of the group of the six qualities, such as mental calm, and so on; and the fourth one is a firm and yearning aspiration for liberation."[1]

---

[1] Śaṅkara, *Vivekacūḍāmaṇi: The Crest Jewel of Discernment, sūtras* 18-19, translation from the Sanskrit and commentary by Raphael (New York: Aurea Vidyā, 2006).

The six qualities described in the *Vivekacūḍāmaṇi* are:

- *śama*, mental calm
- *dama*, self-control
- *uparati*, absorption inwardly
- *titikṣā*, the moral courage that accompanies a spiritual Ideal
- *śraddhā*, faith
- *samādhana*, mental stability, steadfastness, decisive and resolute perseverance.

In the following *sūtras* there is a description of these qualities.

The duties inherent in one's own stage refer to the four *āśramas* of the brahmanic existence: the student stage (*brahmacārya*), the stage of the householder (*gṛhasthya*), the stage of anchorite (*vānaprasthya*) and the stage of total renunciation (*saṁnyāsa*).

The duties inherent to the social class (*varṇa*) refer to the four traditional social orders: *brāhmana*, *kṣatriya*, *vaiśya* and *śūdra*.[1]

brahmādisthāvarānteṣu vairāgyaṁ viṣayeṣvanu ǀ
yathaiva kākaviṣṭāyāṁ vairāgyaṁ tad dhi nirmalam ǁ 4 ǁ

4. *As one is indifferent to a crow's excrement, likewise one must be indifferent to all sensible objects that engender enjoyment, from those of the* Brahmaloka *to*

[1] This division of the *varṇas* is already found in the *Puruṣasūkta* (Hymn to the *Puruṣa*) in the *Ṛg Veda* X.90.

those of this world, because of their transient nature. This [indifference-detachment], in truth, is called pure vairāgya.

Vairāgya is detachment from transient and relative things, cause of conflict and pain. It is a mental habit and should not be intended as inhibition, abandon or absenteeism, and so on, which do not lead to a realizative solution. Detachment is the natural result of discrimination between real and non-real.

When we comprehend that a datum no longer has a raison d'être, we naturally detach from it.

In the *Yoga Vedānta*, *vairāgya* follows the meditated recognition of reality as Unity, and this results in transcending and abandoning the simple mental *representation* of that reality. Even *Brahmaloka* (Paradise) can constitute a reason for bondage; in it one experiences subtler sensible data, but still data. We can, therefore, infer the existence of duality, that is to say, of non-perfection.

But it is necessary, however, that such a sphere as principal Cause, with all that this sphere produces, i.e., the manifestation, be integrated to avoid creating duality (objective Reality-world), whereby the realization would not be completely accomplished.

It is the *guṇas-prakṛti*, not their objects, that imprison the being; detachment represents the condition in which things are not constraining us any longer, but rather it is the being itself that, consciously, dominates things.

nityam ātmasvarūpaṁ hi dṛśyaṁ tadviparītagam |
evaṁ yo niścayaḥ samyagviveko vastunaḥ sa vai || 5 ||

5. *The* ātman *is the sole permanent,* [*while*] *the seen is all that is superimposed on it. This recognition is the fruit of true discrimination-discernment.*

Yogic discrimination aims at recognizing the absolute, the universally valid, the invariable, the ultimate constant that is concealed in the transient and relative factors of the visible. If every relative phenomenon presupposes an inevitable a-causal factor, or a foundation, in which it finds its justification and its meaning only when they are referred to this foundation, then the task of true research of the being should be that of pursuing the supreme Reality.

Now, if the individual has the intellective capability to comprehend the multiplicity of sensible data, he cannot but recognize that the Entity (*ātman*) is the only *permanent*, *constant* and *real* and all the rest (the seen) is nothing but "appearance-phenomenon" (*māyā*).

Summa pax can be realized only where there is a stable, unconditioned and imperishable reality. It is necessary to comprehend whether we are for supreme Fullness or for the simple psychological quiet of the moment.

> "Since those are the philosophers who are able to grasp the realities, which are always unchanging and identical to themselves, while those who have not this capacity are not philosophers because they wander between many realities that are in all sorts of ways..."[1]

---

[1] Plato, *The Republic* VI.484a. See *Politéia* in *Platone: Tutti gli scritti*, edited by G. Reale (Milan: Bompiani [Italian edition], 2000).

sadaiva vāsanātyāgaḥ śamo 'yam iti śabditaḥ |
nigraho bāhyavṛttīnāṁ dama ityabhidhīyate || 6 ||

6. Śama [*calm of mind*] *is the effect of the abandonment of desires, and* dama *the* [*ensuing*] *control of the workings of the vital organs.*

Each desire is something unaccomplished and is born from a dissatisfaction, from a sensory instability and from a subconsciousness (*saṁskāra*) not pacified. Desire fulfills and attenuates fleetingly a mind unable to comprehend, to find its own composure and measure; desire is a simple escape from one's own incompleteness. That one who has reached the "center" ceases to desire because he has found his own fullness. True joy is a calm saturated with omnicomprehensive steadiness. The functions of the sensory organs, i.e., contact with external sensible data, can occur without inhibitions when the psychic aspect (desire) has been resolved. The Liberated can produce action without being constrained by the motivating energies (the three *guṇas*) and by the very effects of the action. The dormant, instead, not only cannot do without acting, but is captive of the very result of that action.

viṣayebhyaḥ parāvṛttiḥ paramoparatir hi sā |
sahanaṁ sarvaduḥkhānāṁ titikṣā sā śubhā matā || 7 ||

7. *The highest self-control* (paramoparatiḥ) *happens when we completely abstract ourselves from sensible objects, while persevering patience in front of any sorrow or pain is known as* titikṣā, *bearer of beatitude.*

If in *śama* and *dama* in order to pacify the extroverted psychic movements a certain effort is needed, in *uparati*, instead, there is a spontaneous concentration in the center of the sensory faculties along with the related abstraction from any sensible datum. These are two stages of a single process of *re-entry*.

nigamācāryavākyeṣu bhaktiḥ śraddheti viśrutā |
cittaikāgryaṁ tu sallakṣye samādhānam iti smṛtam || 8 ||

8. *Faith in the words of the* Vedas *and the Masters [who interpret them] is known as* śraddha, *while concentration of the mind on* sat *[Being] is considered* samādhāna.

Faith springs from an evident and intuitive recognition: the relative presupposes the absolute, the phenomenon the noumenon, impermanence permanence; therefore, to have faith in the absolute does not constitute an emotional, irrational or nonsensical event.

The *Vedas* deal with not only the relative empirical, but also the supreme Reality.

A steady and constant meditation on the real-absolute represents *samādhāna*. This, constantly practiced, unveils the concealed or ultimate reality of things.

saṁsārabandhanirmuktiḥ kathaṁ me syāt kadā vidhe |
iti yā sudṛḍhā buddhir vaktavyā sā mumukṣutā || 9 ||

9. *O Lord, when and how will I be freed from* saṁsāra *[becoming]? Such ardent aspiration is called* mumukṣutā, *or yearning for Liberation.*

When the disciple is intensely burning with love for the Truth, for the Supreme, when he has a single and constant aspiration, that of finding himself in himself, then he is ready for *vairāgya* and the other *sādhanās*.

uktasādhanayuktena vicāraḥ puruṣeṇa hi |
kartavyo jñānasiddhyartham ātmanaḥ śubham icchatā || 10 ||

10. *Only an individual who possesses these qualifications* [*as presuppositions for knowledge*], *and who turns to his own good, will know how to meditate constantly to unveil the Knowledge of the* ātman.

The qualifications required by the neophyte are *only* presuppositions for a correct psychological position and a correct directional start. Often one approaches realization without any qualification, and this is the cause of sure lack of success and frustration.

notpadyate vinā jñānaṁ vicāreṇānyasādhanaiḥ |
yathā padārthabhānaṁ hi prakāśena vinā kvacit || 11 ||

11. *As the perception of an object is determined by light, so knowledge is realized only by means of* vicāra.

If *avidyā* is the cause of our darkness and the veiling of our consciousness, then only the knowledge, through *vicāra* (quest, investigation), can give back to us our authentic condition of being what we are. Neither a blind and passive faith, nor a static ritualism for acquiring merits, nor any type of virtuous action, nor an interested adoration for the creating Entities, can give back to us our integral solution.

"...there they lie deeply concealed... Ignorance, in truth, is destructible, while knowledge, in truth, is immortal. But that One, which controls knowledge and ignorance, is other [from them]"[1]

Advaita Vedānta resolves the problem of the empirical being through *vicāra* that leads to knowledge, which, in its turn, resolves metaphysical ignorance-*avidyā*, *avidyā* that veils the supreme Reality, that which is beyond the entire manifestation enfolded in various degrees and states of consciousness.

Sleep—which is the clouding of our discriminating faculty and the conditioning that makes us appear different from what we are—constitutes the *avidyā-māyā*-appearance, the darkening veil that must be rent with the correct comprehension of the phenomenon.

Between being (becoming) and Non-being as pure and absolute Being exists this veil-sleep-*māyā*, which must be burned by the fire of knowledge-awakening.

ko 'haṁ katham idaṁ jātaṁ ko vai kartā 'sya vidyate |
upādānaṁ kim astīha vicāraḥ so 'yam īdṛśaḥ || 12 ||

12. *Who am I? How did this world unveil? What is its first cause? Of what substance is it made? This is [the investigating method]* vicāra.

This *sūtra* expounds in detail *vicāra*, the method of investigation. It is a philosophical method, a process

[1] *Śvetāśvatara Upaniṣad* V.1, in *Upaniṣad*, edited by Raphael (Milan: Bompiani [Italian edition], 2010).

of pure research of the universals, but, unlike what one might think, it is "experimental."

The *yoga* philosophy is direct experiencing (*anubhava*); only later the mind intervenes to conceptualize as much as possible and to give these concepts, as object of stimulation, to those who desire to facilitate their own experience. Therefore it does not represent an exclusively theoretical process for building a "theory of reality."

Advaita Vedānta, through certain techniques such as *vicāra*, *vairāgya*, *uparati*, etc., offers the opportunity to experience truth, and not simply to think about it or metallize it into simple conceptualizations.

The reality, or the thing in itself, cannot be *object* of ideations; therefore, the *advaita sādhaka*, through *vicāra*, can unveil it.

So, regarding the question: Who am I? it is not sufficient to formulate a simple concept-idea to satisfy the mind of relations; what is necessary is *experiencing* that entity who in fact is asking the question and is behind any possible objectified concept. The conceptual knowledge, however, can have its own preliminary validity.

The questions of *sūtra* 12 are those that the human being, eastern and western, has posed to himself since the beginning of time, giving himself answers of various kinds.

The East of the *Veda-Upaniṣads*, hence of the ancient *ṛsi* (seers), has given responses that, through rituality, lead to the causal Principle (ontological state) and, through buddhic knowledge, or *noesis*, lead to the supreme unborn Reality (supraontological state), i.e., to the *Brahman saguṇa* and to the *nirguṇa*.

The *Veda-Upaniṣads* culminate in the supreme knowledge (*paramārtha*), interiorizing which actualizes the well-known *vākya* "*Tat tvam asi*: You the *jīva* (Soul) are That"; namely, you the entity, fallen into *saṁsāra* (historic becoming), are of the same nature of the supraontological supreme Being, which corresponds to the Being of Parmenides, to the One Good of Plato and to the One of Plotinus. See the teaching of the *Bṛhadāraṇyaka* and *Chāndogya upaniṣads*, of the *Māṇḍūkyakārikā*, etc.; hence the non-dual (*advaita*) *Vedānta* or the One-without-a-second.

nāhaṁ bhūtagaṇo deho nāhaṁ cākṣagaṇas tathā ।
etadvilakṣaṇaḥ kaścid vicāraḥ so 'yam īdṛśaḥ ॥ 13 ॥

13. *I cannot be the gross body with its [five] elements nor the aggregate of the senses: I am something different. This is the* vicāra *method.*

Thus we have two data: the perceiver and the perceived object; this one is born, grows and dies, the other is eternal, because all the perceivable, in its various modifications, represents a simple phenomenon, while the ultimate subject who perceives remains always constant.

ajñānaprabhāvaṁ sarvaṁ jñānena pravilīyate ।
saṁkalpo vividhaḥ kartā vicāraḥ so 'yam īdṛśaḥ ॥ 14 ॥

14. *All things [conceptual representations] are the products of* ajñāna *(non-knowledge), and it is through* jñāna *(knowledge) that they dissolve. The manifold* (vividhaḥ) *[objects] are mental projections. This is the* vicāra *method.*

If we investigate the nature of the sensory object, it can be recognized as the product of the mind. We can note this experience in a clear way in sleep-dream.

In the oneiric condition, the mind has the ability to project the object-subject as well as to be sensitive to its various modifications. That is a true and real event for the dreamer, and no theory is necessary in order to demonstrate it. In dreams the mind generates entire universes (multiplicity) and can experience them sensorially.

Now, *Vedānta* investigation consists in comprehending this entire process of activity and in bringing it back to its right perspective.

etayor yad upādānam ekaṁ sūkṣmaṁ sadavyayam |
yathaiva mṛdghaṭādīnāṁ vicāraḥ so 'yam īdṛśaḥ || 15 ||

15. *As the clay is the substantial cause of the vase, so these two [formal ignorance-thought] are the reflection of the subtle* sat *[ungraspable through the senses] always identical to itself. This is the* vicāra *method.*

aham eko 'pi sūkṣmaś ca jñātā sākṣī sadavyayaḥ |
tad ahaṁ nātra saṁdeho vicāraḥ so 'yam īdṛśaḥ || 16 ||

16. *Because I am also the subtle One, the Knower, the Witness, the unchanging Existent, so, without doubt, "I am That*[1] [Brahman]." *This is the* vicāra *method.*

Because the absolute *Sat* cannot be but one and undivided, we ourselves, as a consequence, are nothing but "That." On the other hand, in that *essence*, what else

[1] *Bṛhadāraṇyaka Upaniṣad* I.IV.10.

could we be if not the Supreme? If in fact we were not, we would create infinite absolutes, and this is contrary to any elementary rationality. Therefore, we are forced to recognize that only the One-without-a-second exists, and this truth is revealed to us not only by rational logic, but also by direct experience, because the immutable supreme Reality is not vacuity.

This recognition clarifies for us the dilemma of duality so much debated by the philosophers. For *Advaita Vedānta,* the object-world surrounding us is *external* to the individual (therefore those who maintain the solipsistic and idealistic absolutism theory, maintaining that the objective world is just a product of our consciousness, are not in agreement with *Advaita Vedānta*) because it is the projection of the Mind (*Mahat*) of *Īśvara*, the principial Entity, the ontological aspect, and in it originate and dissolve all manifest things (see *sūtra* VI of the *Māṇḍūkya Upaniṣad*); analogously, the individualized mind, as we have seen, projects and reabsorbs its ideations. But, at the same time, since in our true essence we are also *Īśvara*, resolving ourselves into It we find ourselves in undivided unity and no longer in duality. Therefore, the objective world is distinct from us (duality) until we overcome the *avidyā-māyā* that, in time-space, separates us from what we really are.

In conclusion, depending on the "position of consciousness" or "point of view" at which we place ourselves, the external world is real (meaning distinct from the perceiving subject) and at the same time non-real because it resolves into Unity.

ātmā viniṣkalo hy eko deho bahubhir āvṛtaḥ ।
tayor aikyaṁ prapaśyanti kim ajñānam ataḥ param ॥ 17 ॥

17. *The* ātman *is one and* [*therefore*] *without parts, while the gross body is simply a compound. Often these two are confused. Can there be greater bewilderment than this?*

If the essence of every thing (multiplicity) is the vital unity, how can we then confuse the elementary or essential with the compound or the manifold? How can we confuse the clay, as essence undivided and identical to itself, with a variously molded form-vase and a simple temporal-spatial phenomenon?

The clay is more than the vase, and we cannot give vase-clay (form-essence) an absolute value of identity, because the vase constitutes only a *moment*-appearance of the clay, as the nocturnal subject-object of the dreamer constitutes a *moment*-appearance of the projecting entity. The clay is the efficient or first cause, although already determined; beyond it, instead, there is the undetermined Infinite.

The error is not in perceiving the object-phenomenon, but in the subsequent phase of identification with the object to the point of *obscuring* the true subject that perceives the object.

ātmā niyāmakaś cāntardeho bāhyo niyamyakaḥ ।
tayor aikyaṁ prapaśyanti kim ajñānam ataḥ param ॥ 18 ॥

18. *The* ātman *is the inner ruler Center, while the body is external and is guided. Often these two are confused. Can there be greater bewilderment than this?*

ātmā jñānamayaḥ puṇyo deho māṁsamayo 'śuciḥ ǀ
tayor aikyaṁ prapaśyanti kim ajñānam ataḥ param ǁ 19 ǁ

19. *The* ātman *is pure knowledge-consciousness, while the body is impure and made of flesh. Often these two are confused. Can there be greater bewilderment than this?*

The *ātman* is imperishable existence self-aware of its being, while the body is a shadow in the desert of life.

> "Before its appearance it [the body] could not exist, and after its disappearance it can never possibly be. Its parabola is just a flash; its qualities are aleatory; it is by nature subject to change. It is made of parts, inert, and, like a jug, is a mere sensory object. Can such a body ever possibly be the *ātman*, the indestructible Witness of all phenomenal changes?"[1]

What is that which, having nothing prior and nothing subsequent, appears to our eyes? What can this datum (the body), having neither a before nor an after, represent? What value can we attribute to something which is in the habit of appearing and disappearing? What wasn't and will not be, can it ever be?

A datum is real because it was, is and always will be; but what wasn't and will not be, how can it be?

---

[1] Śaṅkara, *Vivekacūḍāmaṇi*, *sūtra* 155, op. cit.

Parmenides states:

"...never can be imposed the existence of things that are not."[1]

ātmā prakāśakaḥ svaccho dehas tāmasa ucyate |
tayor aikyaṁ prapaśyanti kim ajñānam ataḥ param || 20 ||

20. *The* ātman *is the enlightener without stain, while the body belongs to darkness. Often these two are confused. Can there be greater bewilderment than this?*

The *ātman* is effulgent self-replendent light in a real sense and not metaphorically, while the body is dark because it lives upon reflected light. The similarity is the same as that of the sun and the earth: the former is pure bright light, the latter is dark and is illuminated and brought into evidence only by the former.

ātmā nityo hi sadrūpo deho 'nityo hy asanmayaḥ |
tayor aikyaṁ prapaśyanti kim ajñānam ataḥ param || 21 ||

21. *The* ātman *is eternal because it is self-existent, the body is transitory because its nature is not real. Often these two are confused. Can there be greater bewilderment than this?*

The *ātman* is eternal because its nature is the same as the supreme *Brahman* constituting the foundation, or the uncaused cause, of the all existent.

---

[1] Parmenides, *On the Order of Nature: For a philosophical ascesis,* fragment 7.1, edited by Raphael (New York: Aurea Vidyā, 2009).

ātmanas tatprakāśatvaṁ yatpadārthavabhāsanam ǀ
nāgnyādidīptivad dīptir bhavaty āndhyaṁ yato niśi ǁ 22 ǁ

22. *The light of the* ātman *reveals all objects, but is not the light of fire or of any other type because* [*with these reflected lights*] *there is always darkness.*

All the vehicles receive the light from the *jīva*, and therefore, from the *ātman*; without the *jīva* the vehicles-bodies could not even exist; and to realize the *ātman*, it is first necessary to realize-integrate the *jīva*.

deho 'ham ity ayaṁ mūḍho dhṛtvā tiṣṭhaty aho janaḥ ǀ
mamāyam ity api jñātvā ghaṭadraṣṭeva sarvadā ǁ 23 ǁ

23. *An individual conditioned by* avidyā *is convinced of being* [*only*] *a body. But the time will come when he will recognize that the body simply belongs to him, just as someone observing a vase.*

Because every entity is a *jīvātman*, it is obvious that sooner or later—both from consciential maturity and impelled by conflicts of various types that force him to reflect and find a solution—the entity will awaken to the recognition of what its real nature is.

brahmaivāhaṁ samaḥ śāntaḥ saccidānandalakṣaṇaḥ ǀ
nāhaṁ deho hy asadrūpo jñānam ity ucyate budhaiḥ ǁ 24 ǁ

24. *Because, in truth, "I am* Brahman," *equanimous and calm, whose nature is Existence-Consciousness-Beatitude. Can I ever be the body that has no real existence? This is the true knowledge of the Sages.*

"I am That: *So 'ham.*" This is the conclusion of *Advaita Vedānta*, and this truth can be self-realized and self-unveiled.

nirvikāro nirākāro niravadyo 'ham avyayaḥ I
nāhaṁ deho hy asadrūpo jñānam ity ucyate budhaiḥ II 25 II

25. *I am devoid of change, form or blame, I am imperishable. Can I ever be the body that has no real existence? This is the true knowledge of the Sages.*

If one wants to see things from the perspective of supreme Reality, it must be recognized that the *ātman,* being of the nature of *Brahman*, is without birth and without death, therefore immutable.[1]

nirāmayo nirābhāso nirvikalpo 'ham ātataḥ I
nāhaṁ deho hy asadrūpo jñānam ity ucyate budhaiḥ II 26 II

26. *I am not subject to illness or fallacious appearance, I am non-mutable and all-pervading. Can I ever be the body that has no real existence? This is the true knowledge of the Sages.*

nirguṇo niṣkriyo nityo nityamukto 'ham acyutaḥ I
nāhaṁ deho hy asadrūpo jñānam ity ucyate budhaiḥ II 27 II

27. *I am devoid of attributes and activity; I am imperishable and always free. Can I ever be the body*

[1] cf. Gauḍapāda, *Māṇḍūkya Upaniṣad* III.19ff, in *Upaniṣad,* edited by Raphael, op. cit

that has no real existence? This is the true knowledge of the Sages.

nirmalo niścalo 'nantaḥ śuddho 'ham ajaro 'maraḥ |
nāhaṁ deho hy asadrūpo jñānam ity ucyate budhaiḥ || 28 ||

28. *I am devoid of all impurity; I am immobile, unlimited, pure, immortal. Can I ever be the body that has no real existence? This is the true knowledge of the Sages.*

svadehe śobhanaṁ santaṁ puruṣākhyaṁ ca saṁmatam |
kiṁ mūrkha śūnyam ātmānaṁ dehātītaṁ karoṣi bhoḥ || 29 ||

29. *O you, taken by* avidyā, *why are you maintaining that the ever-existent and resplendent* ātman, *which resides in your own corporeal aggregate and even beyond it, which is mentioned as* Puruṣa *and established [on the* Śruti], *is non-existent?*

There are some philosophical currents that maintain that everything is relative, impermanent, vacuous, thereby disowning the intimate reality of the entity.

Now, without a perceiver we cannot speak of a perceived thing. Therefore, if we analyze the world of phenomenal duality, we arrive certainly at the experience of relativity; but it remains obvious that this must be perceived by a witness, otherwise we would be faced with the following absurdity and untenable conclusion: the relative becomes absolute or, even, the becoming is perceived by a non-existent entity.

Any type of movement and phenomenal impermanence can be perceived and known from a constant position.

When the mind tries to grasp the ultimate cause of things, an infinitely regressive analysis follows, but without a witness we cannot speak of anything whatsoever of analysis or regression or perception.

It follows, and necessarily so, that there must always be a reality that transcends everything and which *Vedānta* designates, as ultimate expression, by the name *ātman-*without-a-second.

svātmānaṁ śṛṇu mūrkha tvaṁ śrutyā yuktyā ca puruṣam ।
dehātītaṁ sadākāraṁ sudurdarśaṁ bhavādṛśaiḥ ॥ 30 ॥

30. *O you, taken by* avidyā, *with the help of the* Śruti *and reasoning, try to comprehend your own* ātman, *the* Puruṣa, *perfect existence, as it is different from the gross body, even if for you it is difficult to realize it [because you think of it as pure vacuity]*.

ahaṁśabdena vikhyāta eka eva sthitaḥ paraḥ ।
sthūlastvanekatāṁ prāptaḥ kathaṁ syād dehakaḥ pumān ॥ 31 ॥

31. *That which with the word "I"* (ahaṁśabdena) *is known as* eka [*Unity*] *is one only and supreme existent, while the gross body constitutes multiplicity. How can, therefore, this body be the* Puruṣa?

ahaṁ draṣṭṛtayā siddho deho dṛśyatayā sthitaḥ ।
mamāyam iti nirdeśāt kathaṁ syād dehakaḥ pumān ॥ 32 ॥

32. *The* ahaṁ *represents the perceiving subject* (draṣṭṛ), *while the body the object of perception* (dṛśya). *We define it as "mine"* [*and possessed by a subject enjoyer*]. *How can, therefore, this body be the* Puruṣa?

ahaṁ vikārahīnas tu deho nityaṁ vikāravān I
iti pratīyate sākṣāt kathaṁ syād dehakaḥ pumān II 33 II

33. *Direct experience demonstrates that the "I"* (ahaṁ, *as* ātman) *is devoid of change, while the body* [*phenomenon*] *undergoes change. How can, therefore, this body be the* Puruṣa?

A relative entity cannot postulate an absolute relativity because he himself is a relative.

yasmāt param iti śrutyā tayā puruṣalakṣaṇam I
vinirṇītaṁ vimūḍhena kathaṁ syād dehakaḥ pumān II 34 II

34. *The Sages have recognized the* [*real*] *nature of the* Puruṣa *in the following passage of the* Śruti: *"...that Being, with respect to which there is nothing higher..."*[1] *How can, therefore, this body be the* Puruṣa?

sarvaṁ puruṣa eveti sūkte puruṣasaṁjñite I
apy ucyate yataḥ śrutyā kathaṁ syād dehakaḥ pumān II 35 II

35. *Further, the* Śruti *in the* Puruṣa Sūkta[2] *states: "All this is truly the* Puruṣa." *How can, therefore, this body be the* Puruṣa?

---

[1] *Śvetāśvatara Upaniṣad* III.9.

[2] *Ṛg Veda* X.90.2.

asaṅgaḥ puruṣaḥ prokto bṛhadāraṇyake 'pi ca ǀ
anantamalasaṁśliṣṭaḥ kathaṁ syād dehakaḥ pumān ǁ 36 ǁ

36. *In the* Bṛhadāraṇyaka Upaniṣad [IV.III.15] *is also said: "The* Puruṣa *is without contact." How can, therefore, this body, maculated by impurities, be the* Puruṣa*?*

tatraiva ca samākhyātaḥ svayaṁjyotir hi pūruṣaḥ ǀ
jaḍaḥ paraprakāśyo 'yaṁ kathaṁ syād dehakaḥ pumān ǁ 37 ǁ

37. *In the same* Upaniṣad [IV.III.14] *it is clearly stated that: "...this* puruṣa *is self-luminous." How can, therefore, this body, which is inert and illuminated by an external agent, be the* Puruṣa*?*

prokto 'pi karmakāṇḍena hy ātmā dehād vilakṣaṇaḥ ǀ
nityaś ca tatphalaṁ bhuṅkte dehapātād anantaram ǁ 38 ǁ

38. *Also the* Karmakāṇda *states that the* ātman [jīvātman] *is completely different from the body, is imperishable because it subsists, enjoying the fruit [of its state] even when the body decays.*

In all these *sūtras* is highlighted the different condition of the *Puruṣa* and that of the gross body.

"...as a pitcher, [the body] is a simple sensory object... its qualities are aleatory; it is by nature subject to mutation; it is composed of parts, is inert, and before its appearance it could not have existed, nor after its disappearance will it ever be... If it is a simple relative, depending on other, how can it be the *ātman*, the universal lawmaker?"[1]

The *jīva* (living Soul) is veiled, obscured by the qualities of the *guṇas*; these have originated a fictional "psychological persona," characterized by the *ahaṁkāra* (sense of the ego), which is in continuous movement (cf. *Maitry Upaniṣad* IV.2), passing through experiences of different natures and qualities on the gross physical-plane. There can be experiences achieved primarily by the self-aware *jīva*; other experiences, instead, are molded only by the *guṇas*, devoid of self-awareness (cf. *Maitry Upaniṣad* III.2).

The *guṇas* are energies of the *prakṛti* of various qualities, characterized by *sattva* (equilibrium-harmony); by *rajas* (activity, movement toward the exterior; it is through *rajas* that the manifestation is brought from potentiality to act); and by *tamas* (darkness, inertia, clouding of the mind, ignorance of one's own nature, *avidyā*).

The universe is an agglomerate of energies that create forms-bodies at various levels of condensation, expressing qualities of various types (*nāma-rūpa*). All this can take place and exist because there is the *jīva* that gives it raison d'être, and as ultimate source there is always the *Brahman-ātman* as founding Cause of all the existent.

liṅgaṁ cānekasaṁyuktaṁ calaṁ dṛśyaṁ vikāri ca |
avyāpakam asadrūpaṁ tat kathaṁ syāt pumān ayam || 39 ||

---

[1] Śaṅkara, *Vivekacūḍāmaṇi*, *sūtras* 155–156, op. cit.

39. *The subtle body consists equally of parts, is unstable, an object of perception, limited and not self-existent by nature. How can, therefore, this body be the* Puruṣa*?*

Vedānta metaphysics distinguishes these states of being that, obviously, can be experienced because they are objects of knowledge, except the last one: the *ātman-Brahman* that represents the self-existent supreme Reality. One can be such Reality, but it cannot be known empirically.

State	Sheaths	Correspondence
Gross body	*Annamayakośa*	Waking (*Viśva*)
Subtle body	*Prāṇāmayakośa* *Manomayakośa* *Vijñānamayakośa*	Dream (*Taijasa*)
Causal body	*Ānandamayakośa*	Deep sleep (*Prājña*)

↓

Jīva

↓

Brahman-ātman

The subtle and causal bodies correspond to two precise states of consciousness, and the dream and dreamless, or deep sleep, conditions are their symbols or analogies.

The *jīva* is the *shadow* of the *ātman* and uses the five body-sheaths in order to express itself on the three universal planes: *Virāṭ* (physical plane, mass, electrical fire), *Hiraṇyagarbha* (subtle plane, energy, solar fire), *Īśvara* (germinal-causal plane, noumenal fire).[1]

In truth, these three levels constitute a single plane; it is a sole "Fire"-light (*Agni*) expressing three existential *dimensions*.

In fact, the *Vedas* speak of a threefold fire: *jaḍa agni*, *vaidyuta agni* and *saura agni*. All is fire-light because actually "God is a consuming fire."[2]

One who experiences these levels discovers them precisely in terms of "fire-light." It is not, therefore, a question of speculating theoretically on these aspects of Being or simply assuming them; it is only necessary for those who so desire and have the right qualifications to train appropriately, as when an astronaut must go to those spheres that are beyond the terrestrial dimension.

The great *ṛṣis*, transcending the threefold universe, discovered that the sheaths-bodies were *resolved*, but a Witness (no longer individualized) to the various trans-

---

[1] For an in-depth review of the three states of Being, see Gauḍapāda, *Māṇḍūkyakārikā: The Metaphysical Path of Vedānta*, translation from the Sanskrit and commentary by Raphael (New York: Aurea Vidyā, 2002), and Raphael, *The Pathway of Non-duality*, in particular the chapter "The Three States of Being," op. cit.

[2] *Deuteronomy* 4:24.

formations and solutions remained. To this *Ens*-Entity without body, qualities, causality, time and space, to this "ever existent" and pure Being—as it was already mentioned—they gave the name *ātman* (see *sūtra* 40).

evaṁ dehadvayād anya ātmā puruṣa īśvaraḥ |
sarvātmā sarvarūpaś ca sarvātīto 'ham avyayaḥ || 40 ||

40. *So, the always-identical-to-itself* ātman—*substratum of the ego* (ahaṁ)—*is different from these two bodies* (deha dvayāt)*; It is the* Puruṣa, Īśvara, *the* ātman *of all things, being present in all forms and transcending the very forms.*

ityātmadehabhāgena prapañcasyaiva satyatā |
yathoktā tarkaśāstreṇa tataḥ kiṁ puruṣārthatā || 41 ||

41. *The statement that the* ātman *is different from the gross body does not with certainty entail maintaining that the reality of the phenomenal world is according to the* Tarkaśāstra. [*Otherwise*] *of what use would the very aims of a human life be?*

The *Tarkaśāstra* constitutes the "science of logic": the *darśanas* like *Nyāya*, *Sāṁkhya* and *Yoga*[1] or the treatises like the ones of the *Lokāyatika*. But the *sūtra* in question refers more than anything to *Sāṁkhya*, which, through *tarka* (logic), arrives only at the polarity of *Prakṛti* and *Puruṣa*, substance and essence, without, however, openly negating Unity.

In a dual, thus contradictory, reality, the four aims of life (*dharma*: fulfillment of duty; *artha*: aspiration to profane prosperity; *kāma*: fulfillment of desire; *mokṣa*: emancipation from metaphysical ignorance) cannot find a steady attainment because in life there is impermanence and conflict without end; we are, therefore, on the plane of relativity. The human being is truly released from all traces of bondage and error only when the One-without-a-second is attained.

ityātmadehabhedena dehātmatvaṁ nivāritam ।
idānīṁ dehabhedasya hy asattvaṁ sphuṭam ucyate ॥ 42 ॥

42. *Thus the thesis that the body represents the* ātman *is negated by the demonstration, precisely, of the*

---

[1] For a general presentation of the six brahmanic *darśanas* (points of view), refer to S. Radhakrishnan, *Indian Philosophy*. For the texts related to *Nyāya*, *Sāṁkhya* and *Yoga*, see, respectively, the *Nyāya Sūtra* of Gautama, the *Sāṁkhyakārikā* of Īśvarakṛṣṇa and the *Yogadarśana* of Patañjali. For the last mentioned, see Patañjali, *The Regal Way to Realization (Yogadarśana)*, translation from the Sanskrit and commentary by Raphael (New York: Aurea Vidyā, 2012).

difference between the ātman *and the body, as the same difference is also considered unreal.*

"...This *ātman* is the Lord of all human beings, the sovereign of all human beings. As all the spokes of a wheel are fixed in the hub and in the rim of the wheel, so in this *ātman* are stabilized all beings, all gods, all worlds..."[1]

caitanyasyaikarūpatvād bhedo yukto na karhicit |
jīvatvaṁ ca mṛṣā jñeyaṁ rajjau sarpagraho yathā || 43 ||

43. *No division of consciousness is possible because [it] is always unique and identical to itself. Also the* ahaṁkāra *must be considered apparent, like a snake superimposed on a rope.*

The changeable contents of the sensorial consciousness can be indefinite, but consciousness remains nonetheless itself and undivided because it represents a shining ray of the consciousness-intelligence of the *jīvātman.*

rajjvajñānāt kṣaṇenaiva yadvad rajjur hi sarpiṇī |
bhāti tadvac citiḥ sākṣād viśvākāreṇa kevalā || 44 ||

44. *As, because of ignorance of the real nature of the rope, the rope for a moment appears as snake, so pure Consciousness, devoid of change, appears as phenomenal universe.*

upādānaṁ prapañcasya brahmaṇo 'nyan na vidyate |
tasmāt sarvaprapañco 'yaṁ brahmaivāsti na cetarat || 45 ||

---

[1] *Bṛhadāraṇyaka Upaniṣad* II.V.15.

45. *The efficient cause of the universe is* Brahman, *whereby this entire universe is nothing but* Brahman.

Brahman is that by which the entire universe, with all that it implies, finds its raison d'être; without That, its own same birth would not be possible.

vyāpyavyāpakatā mithyā sarvam ātmeti śāsanāt |
iti jñāte pare tattve bhedasyāvasaraḥ kutaḥ || 46 ||

46. *From the statement of the* Śruti: "Brahman *is Self-existent"* [Bṛhadāraṇyaka Upaniṣad IV.VI.3] *follows that the idea of perceiver and perceived* [*duality*] *is illusory. That reality* [Brahman *is all*] *once realized, where can there be the distinction between cause and effect?*

There are some theories that maintain that the effect is different from the cause (*ārambhavāda*), other ones that the cause changes into the effect (*pariṇāmavāda*).

Only the *vivartavāda* has the courage to draw the ultimate conclusions: all the phenomenal is neither real nor unreal, it is simply appearance.[1]

"...this *Kṣatra*, these worlds, these Gods, these beings: all this is nothing but *ātman*."[2]

---

[1] For a broader explanation of these philosophical doctrines, see Gauḍapāda, *Māṇḍūkyakārikā*, op. cit., and Raphael, *The Pathway of Non-duality*, op. cit.

[2] *Bṛhadāraṇyaka Upaniṣad* IV.V.7.

"That is Fullness, this is fullness.
Fullness derives from Fullness.
Drawn fullness from Fullness,
still Fullness remains."[1]

The fullness of the sensible is nothing but a "shadow" of that of the intelligible.

śrutyā nivāritaṁ nūnaṁ nānātvaṁ svamukhena hi |
kathaṁ bhāso bhaved anyaḥ sthite cādvayakāraṇe || 47 ||

47. *The* Śruti *has directly negated differentiation. If non-duality is a demonstrated fact, how can appearance [universe] be regarded as real?*

"Only with the mind [*buddhi*] It must be known. In That there is no multiplicity. Goes from death to death one who here sees only multiplicity."[2]

If we reflect on the real nature of Unity, we must necessarily acknowledge that it is devoid of parts, without distinctions and fragmentation. If, then, unity does not have a second with which to measure itself or to contrapose, whence may originate the concepts of duality and cause-effect?

That which we empirically observe and which we erroneously consider dual cannot have any valid founda-

---

[1] *Īśa Upaniṣad,* "Invocation." See *Five Upaniṣads*: *Īśa, Kaivalya, Sarvasāra, Amṛtabindu, Atharvaśira*, translation from the Sanskrit and commentary by Raphael (New York: Aurea Vidyā, forthcoming).

[2] *Bṛhadāraṇyaka Upaniṣad* IV.IV.19.

tion precisely because differentiation only appears in the empirical dimension.

doṣo 'pi vihitaḥ śrutyā mṛtyor mṛtyuṁ sa gacchati |
iha paśyati nānātvaṁ māyayā vañcito naraḥ || 48 ||

48. *The* Śruti *has again condemned diversity when it states: "Goes from death to death one who here sees only multiplicity."*[1]

brahmaṇaḥ sarvabhūtāni jāyante paramātmanaḥ |
tasmād etāni brahmaiva bhavantīty avadhārayet || 49 ||

49. *Because all entities come from* Brahman, [*that is*] *the supreme* ātman, *they must recognize that they are verily* Brahman.

The snake that one sees in place of the rope is not distinct from the rope; in reality it is the very rope seen under the veil of *māyā*. Thus the entire universe is considered real-absolute because it is seen under the veil of *avidyā*; but when the veil is removed, the universe results as a simple phenomenon that appears and disappears on the horizon of the supreme Witness.

brahmaiva sarvanāmāni rūpāṇi vividhāni ca |
karmāṇy api samagrāṇi bibhartīti śrutir jagau || 50 ||

50. *The* Śruti *has clearly stated that* Brahman *is the only substratum of the world of names, of forms and of every action.*

---

[1] Ibid.

Brahman is the screen upon which are woven the chiaroscuros of existence and constitutes the foundation of both noumenon and phenomenon, and therefore the metaphysical foundation of Being and becoming.

suvarṇāj jāyamānasya suvarṇatvaṁ ca śāśvatam ׀
brahmaṇo jāyamānasya brahmatvaṁ ca tathā bhavet ׀׀ 51 ׀׀

51. *As an object produced from gold has always the nature of gold, so* [*an* ens *that appears*] *generated from* Brahman *has always the nature* [*of* Brahman].

svalpam apy antaraṁ kṛtvā jīvātmaparamātmanoḥ ׀
yaḥ saṁtiṣṭhati mūḍhātmā bhayaṁ tasyābhibhāṣitam ׀׀ 52 ׀׀

52. *Fear is attributed* [*by the* Śruti] *to the uncultivated one who distinguishes the* jīvātman *from the* paramātman.

Fear originates from a sense of "passing out," of "feeling lost," of imagining that an event may be prejudicial. This feeling, though, represents an illusory state because Being, which is immortal, indestructible and eternally fulfilled, can neither pass out nor be impaired, conditioned or stained by any possible action and sensorial duality.

Fear is the defense of the ego-*ahaṁkāra*, but precisely this movement denotes its weakness and vulnerability. Fear is irrational because the ego itself is irrational, and when it appears living in certainty and security, it is only because certain actions or circumstances seem reliable. But that certainty and security are always of the emotional sphere, whose nature is *movement*, and therefore conflict.

From a metaphysical point of view, the individual, identifying with his own shadow of incompleteness, cannot but be subjected to the agonizing feeling of fear. Only the reality is completeness and perfect harmony, and only by living the reality can the individual transcend every "feeling of...."

"But until he projects even the slightest difference within This, then for him fear subsists."[1]

yatrājñānād bhaved dvaitam itaras tatra paśyati I
ātmatvena yadā sarvaṁ netaras tatra cāṇv api II 53 II

53. *When because of ignorance duality arises, one sees* [*the other*], *but when all is resolved into the* ātman, *then the One cannot see* [*the second*].

"In truth, where there is duality, there one sees the other, one sniffs the other... one thinks of the other... one knows the other. But when, for him, all has become his own very *ātman*, then through what means and what will it be possible to see?... Through what will it be possible to know That thanks to which all is known?"[2]

yasmin sarvāṇi bhūtāni hy ātmatvena vijānataḥ I
na vai tasya bhaven moho na ca śoko 'dvitīyataḥ II 54 II

---

[1] *Taittirīya Upaniṣad* II.VII.1.

[2] *Bṛhadāraṇyaka Upaniṣad* IV.V.15.

54. *When identity with the* ātman *is realized, there is no* [*more*] *delusion or pain, by lack, precisely, of duality.*

> "In that [state], when the knowledge of the *ātman* has become all the beings, what bewilderment, what affliction [can there be] for that one who recognizes himself as [supreme] unity?"[1]

The cause of pain and conflictual incompleteness is the fragmentation of oneself in that ego (*ahaṁkāra*), is the dismemberment of one's unity. This precarious dispersion of consciousness provokes resistances, therefore suffering.

The individual lives in conflict because he has not *rediscovered* himself, he has not resolved his scissure.

ayam ātmā hi brahmaiva sarvātmakatayā sthitaḥ |
iti nirdhāritaṁ śrutyā bṛhadāraṇyasaṁsthayā || 55 ||

55. *The* Śruti, *through the* Bṛhadāraṇyaka, *declares that this* ātman, *which is the Whole, is really* Brahman.

> "That is this *Brahman*, without antecedent or subsequent, without internal and without external: this *ātman*, through which all is known, is *Brahman*. This is the teaching."[2]

anubhūto 'py ayaṁ loko vyavahārakṣamo 'pi san |
asadrūpo yathā svapna uttarakṣaṇabādhataḥ || 56 ||

56. *This world, although experienced in all its own empirical finalities, belongs, as the dream world, to the*

[1] *Īśa Upaniṣad* 7.

[2] *Bṛhadāraṇyaka Upaniṣad* II.V.19.

nature of non-existence, because it is always contradicted by successive moments.

svapno jāgaraṇe 'līkaḥ svapne 'pi jāgaro na hi I
dvayam eva laye nāsti layo 'pi hy ubhayor na ca II 57 II

57. [*The experience*] *of the dream remains unreal in the waking condition, as* [*the experience*] *of waking proves non-real in the dream state. Neither of them exists in the state of deep sleep, which, in its turn, cannot exist in the first two states.*

trayam evaṁ bhaven mithyā guṇatrayavinirmitam I
asya draṣṭā guṇātīto nityo hy ekaś cidātmakaḥ II 58 II

58. *Thus, the three conditions are non-real since they are simple modifications of the three* guṇas, *but the Witness one and eternal* [*through which the all can be perceived*] *is beyond the three* guṇas; *it is the* ātman [*in that*] *pure Intelligence* (cidātma).

In the last three *sūtras* is enunciated the *Vedānta* cosmogony and its right positioning in the grand scheme of things.

The three macrocosmic states are the following:

Virāṭ	Gross state	1st *pāda*	Waking
Hiraṇyagarbha	Subtle state	2nd *pāda*	Dream
Īśvara or *Brahma*	Causal state	3rd *pāda*	Deep sleep
Brahman-Turīya		The Fourth	

They are nothing but vibratory modalities, modifications within *saguṇa Brahman* or *Īśvara*, the ontological aspect; the sole supreme Reality is *nirguṇa Brahman* or *Turīya*.[1] According to the point of view from which one looks at them, they can be real or non-real. Why this paradoxical contradiction? A datum is real or is not real, the contradiction introduced in the principle leading to annulment of the very principle.

To comprehend the paradox, it is well to clarify some fundamental points of *Vedānta* metaphysics, which, as we know, concerns the science of the first Principles, the ultimate truth of things, the essence or the foundation underlying every datum, the *constant* everywhere; in other words, the unconditioned-Absolute as such. It represents the One-One of Plato.[2]

The instrument of cognitive approach is the supraconscious intuition, the synthetic mind, pure reason or the higher intellect (*buddhī*). We can say that, in descending order, physics follows metaphysics as the science of the empirical, the changing phenomenon, the condensed energies and so on.

We have, therefore, two points of view: one of universal order, synthetic, noumenal and essential; the other of particular order, individual or general (non-universal). It

---

[1] cf. Gauḍapāda, *Māṇḍūkyakārikā*, op. cit.

[2] cf. Raphael, *Initiation into the Philosophy of Plato*, in particular the chapter "Platonism and *Vedānta*," in which are compared the doctrines of Plato and Śaṅkara (New York: Aurea Vidyā, 2005).

is obvious that these two perspectives, if taken separately, can be contradictory and, as such, reciprocally annulling.

One who is *exclusively* anchored or identified with the empirical point of view is constrained to see things empirically, distinctively and selectively, while a metaphysician cannot but see them in terms of noumenal, universal, of unity and of constant.

The empiricists consider the metaphysicians as "fantastic," "evasive" and outside of reality; these, in their turn, point out to the empiricists that they are investigating and considering as absolute an evanescent transitoryness: as soon as they define a datum, it has already disappeared from their hands as a mirage in the desert. The empiricists are children who want to seize in their own hands... the air, the fog surrounding them.

A *true* metaphysician, positioning himself in a more synthetic and universal state, cannot but comprehend the empiricist, while often and for obvious reasons, the empiricist does not comprehend the metaphysician.

The *Vedānta* position, as the saying goes, "cuts off the head of the bull," arriving at a truly all-encompassing vision avoiding irrational extremisms created by a mind unable to comprehend. What is *Advaita Vedānta* saying? The motion-universe (the three states mentioned earlier) can be considered as real or as non-real, depending upon whether the perspective is empirical or metaphysical. But, we could also ask ourselves, is there not a sole reality always identical to itself and universally valid? It is true, this reality is, and cannot not be (even a hardened nihilist has his own reality that corresponds to the "nil"), and it is one only; but the supreme Reality does not represent a "point of view" because it is the *Foundation* of all that exists, that receives *esse* from That.

If there is a philosophy that is more acceptable and more adherent to the empirical mentality, this certainly is *Vedānta*. The *Vedānta darśana* has a vision that is synthetic, metaphysical, sapiential, and, as we were saying before, not extremist: it renders to Caesar that which is Caesar's and to *Brahman* that which is *Brahman's*.

Śaṅkara maintains: for someone who in the rope sees a snake, the snake is real; while for someone who sees the rope and nothing but the rope, the snake vanishes, and if someone talks about a snake, he considers him the victim of some kind of delusion, of *avidyā*.

Therefore we have that from an empirical point of view, the object-universe can be considered real; but if we move the perspective to the metaphysical sphere, it is nothing but a mirage in the desert, as Gauḍapāda demonstrates in his *kārikās* to the *Māṇḍūkya Upaniṣad*.

The three *sūtras* in question enunciate a purely metaphysical postulate: the three states (*māyā*, conformed movement) are non-real because they contradict one another and do not represent that *constant*, which must constitute the true characteristic of the Real as such.

For Śaṅkara, the Being-reality is such if it remains constant, always identical to itself, not dependent on other being-reality and is devoid of contradiction; it must therefore possess the characteristics of ultimate truth, of identity, of universality (not generality) and of unity. Here is the statement of *sūtra* 56: "This world... belongs, as the world of dream, to the nature of non-existence, because it is always contradicted by successive moments."

In other words, it is not constant, identical, One. The Being-reality represents the One-Good of Plato, the One of Plotinus and the Being of Parmenides, to mention some metaphysicians.[1] However, the relative and the constant should be integrated into the supreme Reality, which is the support of both cognitive factors.

yadvan mṛdi ghaṭabhrāntiṁ śuktau vā rajatasthitim ǀ
tadvad brahmaṇi jīvatvaṁ vīkṣamāṇe na paśyati ǀǀ 59 ǀǀ

59. *As a person does not mistake, once the illusion vanishes, a mother-of-pearl for a piece of silver or a piece of clay for a jug, so, similarly, by realizing* Brahman, *all* jīvas *resolve themselves [in* Brahman].

When we are veiled by *avidyā,* we recognize ourselves as individuality separate from *Brahman*, but when the realization-knowledge unveils, then we recognize ourselves as *Brahman*-without-a-second.

For *Vedānta*, we have said, knowledge is of a realizative order, not a speculative-learned-discursive end in itself. *Brahman* is not an object of knowledge, but a Reality to be unveiled consciously.

yathā mṛdi ghaṭo nāma kanake kuṇḍalābhidhā ǀ
śuktau hi rajatakhyātir jīvaśabdas tathā pare ǀǀ 60 ǀǀ

---

[1] For an in-depth study of this subject, see Raphael, *Initiation into the Philosophy of Plato*, in particular the chapter "The One-Good as Metaphysical Reality," op. cit., and Parmenides, *On the Order of Nature,* in particular the chapter "Being," op. cit.

60. *As clay is considered a jug, gold an earring and mother-of-pearl silver, so* Brahman *is considered* jīva.

yathaiva vyomni nīlatvaṁ yathā nīraṁ marusthale I
puruṣatvaṁ yathā sthāṇau tadvad viśvaṁ cidātmani II 61 II

61. *As we see blue in the sky, water in a mirage and a human figure where there just is a pole, so we see the universe in place of* Brahman-ātman.

yathaiva śūnye vetālo gandharvāṇāṁ puraṁ yathā I
yathākāśe dvicandratvaṁ tadvat satye jagat sthitiḥ II 62 II

62. *As we see an image where there is none, a castle hanging in the air or a second moon in the sky [as simple mental representations], so we see the universe where, instead, there is only* Brahman.

yathā taraṅgakallolair jalam eva sphuraty alam I
pātrarūpeṇa tāmraṁ hi brahmāṇḍaughais tathātmatā II 63 II

63. *As water appears as wave or spray and copper in the form of a pot, so the* ātman-Brahman *appears universe* (aṇḍa, *the cosmic egg that contains the universe*).

ghaṭanāmnā yathā pṛthvī paṭanāmnā hi tantavaḥ I
jagannāmnā cid ābhāti jñeyaṁ tat tad abhāvataḥ II 64 II

64. *As clay appears with the name of [any] container or a [cotton] thread appears under the name of a piece of cloth, so That* (tad) *appears under the name of the universe. To realize the* ātman (tat) *it is necessary to transcend the appearance of names and forms.*

By eliminating names and forms (*abhava*: "what is non-real" in the *sūtra*) erroneously superimposed on the *ātman*, the *ātman* unveils in its purity and uniqueness. In these *sūtras* is demonstrated Śaṅkara's theory of superimpositions (*adhyāsa*).

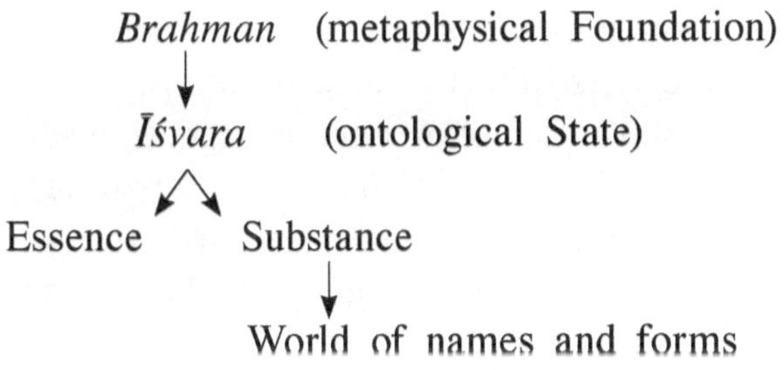

sarvo 'pi vyavahāras tu brahmaṇā kriyate janaiḥ |
ajñānān na vijānanti mṛdeva hi ghaṭādikam || 65 ||

65. *Human beings experience in* Brahman *and through* Brahman [*and do not know it*], *precisely as through ignorance they do not comprehend that* [*after all*] *jugs and other vases* [*that one handles*] *are nothing but clay.*

We cannot consider the snake as distinct from the rope: the former is just a particular mental representation of the latter and is devoid of an intrinsic existence of its own. The universe is a particularized image of *Brahman* and can be conceptualized precisely because there is *Brahman* as support.

kāryakāraṇatā nityam āste ghaṭamṛdor yathā ।
tathaiva śrutiyuktibhyāṁ prapañcabrahmaṇor iha ॥ 66 ॥

66. *Between the clay and the vase there is a tight relationship, as between* Brahman *and the phenomenal universe. This is stated by the Scriptures and validated by reasoning.*

As the various vases are nothing but a simple modification of clay, so the universe is nothing but the light-shadow or reflection of *Brahman saguṇa* itself. And as the various vases are not distinct or separate from the clay, whereby we cannot speak of birth in the sense of *coming out,* so the light-shadow is not separate from *Brahman saguṇa.*

gṛhyamāṇe ghaṭe yadvan mṛttikā 'yāti vai balāt ।
vīkṣamāṇe prapañce 'pi brahmaivābhāti bhāsuram ॥ 67 ॥

67. *As contemplating a vase we can perceive* [*suddenly*] *the clay, so contemplating the phenomenon-world we can perceive the ever-resplendent* Brahman saguṇa.

There are moments in which contemplating a phenomenon one can grasp the noumenon, the underlying reality, the ever-constant substratum. With persevering practice of spiritual discrimination or discernment, one gradually arrives at eliminating all attributes superimposed onto *Brahman*. One also discovers that the space-time qualities have no autonomous and absolute reality, but represent *ideations* of the various *manas* involved in the relationship.

"...thus, after that, there is a description [of *Brahman*] as: 'not this, not this' (*neti neti*), because, in truth, there is no better [indication] other than: 'not this.'"[1]

To those who are incapable of meditating on the *Brahman* without attributes, it is suggested concentrating on certain qualities that are normally superimposed on it, making meditation easier; then slowly it is necessary to eliminate all attributes, from the grosser to the subtler: in this way one gradually arrives at realizing the undifferentiated *Brahman nirguṇa*.

The Absolute, as it is beyond time, space and causality, cannot be apprehended, obviously, through empirical means, cannot be meditated upon or known through objects; it is the imperishable Witness-without-a-second. If *Brahman* could be known through any attribute, it would cease to be the unconditioned *Brahman* and would become a simple attribute-object of the mind.

The *Brahman nirguṇa*, or *Brahma* (neuter), is the foundation of the existent totality, and therefore it is beyond cause-effect and time-space. The *Brahman saguṇa*, or *Brahmā* (masculine), is the state of Being, the ontological state, the Cause of manifestation. In platonic terms the *Brahman* can be equated to the One-Good, the supra-ontological state, and the *Brahmā* to the "World of Ideas," the ontological state; for Plotinus as well there is the same comparison with the One, the supra-ontological state, and the *Noûs*, the supreme primordial Intelligence, which gives origin to the manifestation.

---

[1] *Bṛhadāraṇyaka Upaniṣad* II.III.6.

Often everything is related to the sole *Brahman* without attributes, because, simplifying the sequence of the various states, it can be agreed that, in the final analysis, it is the *Brahman nirguṇa* that gives the *esse* to *Brahmā* and, as a consequence, to the manifestation itself. In fact, *Brahman* literally means "growth," "expansion," that which provides the possibility of "development," of manifesting. Besides, the *ātman*, referring to the human entity, is considered by the *Śruti* in identity with *Brahman*, thereby the two terms interchanged.

The traditional Orient, which is less empirical than the Occident, often attributes to *Brahman* every kind of reference, including that of the birth of manifestation, but then it clarifies—in many doctrinal contexts—that *Brahman* is beyond attributes, beyond action, and therefore non-agent, and in the *Māṇḍūkya Upaniṣad* it is clarified that *Brahman* is non-born, thus considering it as the foundation or the founding cause of all:

> "But when the mind has dissolved and there remains [only] the Beatitude of which the *ātman* is *Witness*, that [state] is the immortal *Brahman*..."[1]

> *Brahman* is:

> "...undefinable (*alakṣana*), unthinkable (*acintya*), indescribable (*avyapadeśya*), ...without any trace of manifestation (*prapañcopaśama*)..."[2]

---

[1] *Maitry Upaniṣad* VI.24.

[2] cf. *Māṇḍūkya Upaniṣad, sūtra* VII.

sadaivātmā viśuddho 'sti hy aśuddho bhāti vai sadā |
yathaiva dvividhā rajjur jñānino 'jñānino 'niśam || 68 ||

68. *The* ātman, *although eternally pure, may seem impure [to the non-Awakened], precisely as a rope may appear in two different ways.*

We were saying elsewhere that, for the Knower, the rope is always so, while for one who is asleep it may appear as snake, garland, staff, etc. (space-time representational points).

So, as indicated earlier, there are two orders of truth: one absolute, constant and universal, which is of metaphysical order, the other of space-time, therefore contingent and transient, both resolving in *Brahman.*

yathaiva mṛnmayaḥ kumbhas tadvad deho 'pi cinmayaḥ |
ātmānātmavibhāgo 'yaṁ mudhaiva kriyate 'budhaiḥ || 69 ||

69. *As a vase is nothing but clay, so the body [of the individual] is nothing but consciousness* (cit). *The duality,* ātman–*non*-ātman (ātmānātma), *is posited only by the non-Knower.*

The dualists think that the body is the *ātman* and that the universe and *Brahman* are two absolutely distinct and separated entities. But how can there be two absolutes? How can there be a divided Unity? Matter-light is one, and all the atomic molecular forms, of any type and degree, are nothing but matter-light at different degrees of condensation or vibration. To consider a form distinct from matter-light, thus creating an irreducible duality, means being misled by the empirical mind.

sarpatvena yathā rajjū rajatatvena śuktikā ।
vinirṇītā vimūḍhena dehatvena tathātmatā ॥ 70 ॥

70. *As a rope is imagined as a snake and a mother-of-pearl as a piece of silver, so the* ātman *is imagined as gross body by people of little intellect.*

ghaṭatvena yathā pṛthvī paṭatvenaiva tantavaḥ ।
vinirṇītā vimūḍhena dehatvena tathātmatā ॥ 71 ॥

71. *As clay is imagined as a vase and the thread [of cotton] as cloth, so the* ātman *is imagined as gross body by people of little intellect.*

kanakaṁ kuṇḍalatvena taraṅgatvena vai jalam ।
vinirṇītā vimūḍhena dehatvena tathātmatā ॥ 72 ॥

72. *As gold is imagined as an earring and water as a wave, so the* ātman *is imagined as gross body by people of little intellect.*

puruṣatvena vai sthāṇur jalatvena marīcikā ।
vinirṇītā vimūḍhena dehatvena tathātmatā ॥ 73 ॥

73. *As the trunk of a tree is imagined as a human form and a simple mirage as water, so the* ātman *is imagined as gross body by people of little intellect.*

gṛhatvenaiva kāṣṭhāni khaḍgatvenaiva lohatā ।
vinirṇītā vimūḍhena dehatvena tathātmatā ॥ 74 ॥

74. *As a quantity of processed wood is imagined as a house and steel as a sword, so the* ātman *is imagined as gross body by people of little intellect.*

yathā vṛkṣaviparyāso jalād bhavati kasyacit |
tadvad ātmani dehatvaṁ paśyaty ajñānayogatāḥ || 75 ||

75. *As a person sees the reflection of a tree in a pool of water, so because of* āvidya *he sees the* ātman *as the body.*

It has often been said that *Brahman* is One-without-a-second, but appears as many and with attributes-qualities that, after all, do not belong to it. Why all this? What is there that determines such a phenomenon?

The ultimate reason of a thing is encompassed in the *nature* of the thing itself, and speculating on the ultimate nature of a datum means not having comprehended the "principle of nature," that is, that nature simply *is*.

Why this nature and not another one? Also with another nature we would ask the same question. This will take us to a *regressio ad infinitum*, characteristic of a mind that does not comprehend.

What determines the passage from Non-Being to the Being, the appearance of the noumenon as phenomenon? *Advaita Vedānta* answers that Non-Being cannot become Being because this would invalidate the Principle, but that *Brahman nirguṇa*, although always remaining the same, appears as *Brahman saguṇa*, qualified through *māyā* at the universal level and *avidyā* at the individual level.

Although *māyā* cannot be defined in its essentiality, nonetheless we know it because we experience it on a daily basis. Besides: although *māyā* is "object of experimentation," it nonetheless has no intrinsic reality of its own, because it itself appears and disappears.

When we observe a rope and it appears as snake, *avidyā-māyā* has brought forth a twofold operation: it has "projected" an image (representation) and the image has superimposed itself on the rope, "veiling" it. These two powers of "projection" (*vikṣepaśakti*) and "veiling" (*āvṛtiśakti*), which belong to *māyā*, operate always in the field of our mind, but it is equally true that when we observe the rope properly and we discover it for what it is, *māyā-avidyā* disappears.[1] We can, therefore, say that *māyā* is impalpable and unseizable precisely because of its evanescent and non-substantial nature.

Prakṛti, which for *Sāṁkhya* constitutes one of the two ultimate realities, the other being constituted by *Puruṣa*, for *Advaita Vedānta* represents *māyā*, a crossroad of light-shadow that makes appear things that in reality are not. So, through *māyā-avidyā*, *Brahman* appears as this or that, the *ātman* appears as body or other; it is sufficient, though, to eliminate the veil so that the *ātman* shows itself in its sole, true and authentic reality. Plato would say: the sensible partakes of the reality of Being, though it is not Being.

potena gacchataḥ puṁsaḥ sarvaṁ bhātīva cañcalam ǀ
tadvad ātmani dehatvaṁ paśyaty ajñānayogataḥ ǁ 76 ǁ

---

[1] For the powers of "projection" and "veiling," see Śaṅkara, *Dṛgdṛśyaviveka:* Discernment between *ātman* and *non-ātman*, in particular *sūtras* 13 and 15, translation from the Sanskrit and commentary by Raphael (New York: Aurea Vidyā, 2008).

76. *As to a person who is sailing all appears as moving, so because of ignorance the* ātman *appears as physical form.*

pītatvaṁ hi yathā śubhre doṣād bhavati kasyacit ।
tadvad ātmani dehatvaṁ paśyaty ajñānayogataḥ ॥ 77 ॥

77. *As to a sick person white things appear as yellow, so because of ignorance the* ātman *appears as physical form.*

cakṣurbhyāṁ bhramaśīlābhyāṁ sarvaṁ bhāti bhramātmakam।
tadvad ātmani dehatvaṁ paśyaty ajñānayogataḥ ॥ 78 ॥

78. *As to a person with defective eye-sight everything appears distorted, so because of ignorance the* ātman *appears as physical form.*

alātaṁ bhramaṇenaiva vartulaṁ bhāti sūryavat ।
tadvad ātmani dehatvaṁ paśyaty ajñānayogataḥ ॥ 79 ॥

79. *As a burning ember, with simple rotation, appears as a circle, so because of ignorance the* ātman *appears as physical form.*

mahattve sarvavastūnām aṇutvaṁ hy atidūrataḥ ।
tadvad ātmani dehatvaṁ paśyaty ajñānayogataḥ ॥ 80 ॥

80. *As, because of distance, large things appear small, so because of ignorance the* ātman *appears as physical form.*

sūkṣmatve sarvabhāvānāṁ sthūlatvaṁ copanetratāḥ ǀ
tadvad ātmani dehatvaṁ paśyaty ajñānayogataḥ ǁ 81 ǁ

81. *As small things, observed through lenses, become large, so because of ignorance the* ātman *appears as physical form.*

kācabhūmau jalatvaṁ vā jalabhūmau hi kācatā ǀ
tadvad ātmani dehatvaṁ paśyaty ajñānayogataḥ ǁ 82 ǁ

82. *As a simple glass surface is believed to be a pool of water or vice versa, so because of ignorance the* ātman *appears as physical form.*

yadvad agnau maṇitvaṁ hi maṇau vā vahnitā pumān ǀ
tadvad ātmani dehatvaṁ paśyaty ajñānayogataḥ ǁ 83 ǁ

83. *As a person imagines a jewel in the fire, so because of ignorance the* ātman *appears as physical form.*

abhreṣu satsu dhāvatsu somo dhāvati bhāti vai ǀ
tadvad ātmani dehatvaṁ paśyaty ajñānayogataḥ ǁ 84 ǁ

84. *As the moon appears moving when the clouds are moving, so because of ignorance the* ātman *appears as physical form.*

yathaiva digviparyāso mohād bhavati kasyacit ǀ
tadvad ātmani dehatvaṁ paśyaty ajñānayogataḥ ǁ 85 ǁ

85. *As a person, because of confusion, loses his bearings, so because of ignorance the* ātman *appears as physical form.*

yathā śaśī jale bhāti cañcalatvena kasyacit ।
tadvad ātmani dehatvaṁ paśyaty ajñānayogataḥ ॥ 86 ॥

86. *As the moon reflected in the water appears vacillating, so because of ignorance the* ātman *appears as physical form.*

evam ātmanyavidyāto dehādhyāso hi jāyate ।
sa evātmaparijñānāl līyate ca parātmani ॥ 87 ॥

87. *So, because of obfuscation of the* jīvātman, *the illusion of the body is born, but through realization [the illusion having vanished] the* ātman *recognizes itself as the Supreme.*

In this group of *sūtras* Śaṅkara highlights three types of error: one on the *nature* of reality itself or *paramārtha* Knowledge, another on the description of anatomy of the event-object and a last one on the erroneous perception derived from the limitation of the sensory means.

The last two errors create an eruditive confusion and obfuscation of the intellect; the first, instead, constitutes true *avidyā,* which is non-awareness of the ultimate nature of the real; in other words, it deals with the nature of Being.

It is well to reiterate the fact that *avidyā* does not represent an ignorance of notions about a specific object, nor is it the lack of scholarly, cultural or other knowledge. *Avidyā* is something more because it refers to the reality of the Being, and *avidyā* can be defeated with its own counterpart, i.e., *vidyā* or noetic knowledge.

A perceptual error occurs when we mistake one color for another, when because of distance large things appear small or distorted, and so on.

An error about the structure of an object occurs when we lack specific descriptive notions. If we do not have the right notion regarding the structure of a molecule, when we try to define it or use it, we fall into error, and this is what constitutes common ignorance, i.e., we ignore the anatomical structure of a phenomenon, an event, etc.

The error, instead, regarding the nature of reality in itself occurs when we mistake Being for non-being, the real for the unreal, the phenomenon for the noumenon, and so on, or vice versa. *Avidyā* concerns precisely this kind of error, as said before.

From all this we can infer that for the last two errors (but primarily for the former), which are about lack of erudition, we find the solution through culture or the correct conceptual-distinctive knowledge (opposition of knowledge-ignorance); while for the first error, which is of metaphysical nature, the solution can no longer be represented by conceptual knowledge, because Reality cannot be expressed through concepts, but by consciential realization.

Avidyā has no correlation on the empirical plane as, strictly speaking, it does not belong to this domain; therefore, it cannot be resolved with the simple empirical-descriptive knowledge of analytical thought.

From these premises we can now comprehend the difference between Sacred Knowledge of the Traditional order, which deals with the nature of Being and therefore with realization, and conceptual knowledge, which consists in deciphering the operational mechanism of the phenomena.

sarvam ātmatayā jñātaṁ jagat sthāvarajaṅgamam I
abhāvāt sarvabhāvānāṁ dehasya cātmatā kutaḥ II 88 II

88. *When the entire universe, immobile and mobile, is known from the point of view of the* ātman *as non-existent* (abhāvat), *how can it be sustained that the body is the* ātman?

Śaṅkara always highlights the non-duality of pure Being to avoid falling into dualism, which to a sensory mind could indeed appear real.

ātmānaṁ satataṁ jānan kālaṁ naya mahād yute I
prārabdham akhilaṁ bhuñjan nodvegaṁ kartum arhasi II 89 II

89. *O you, great enlightened, who are continuously in contemplation of the* ātman, *do not feel disquiet while you spend time experiencing the fruits of* prārabdha.

utpanne 'py ātmavijñāne prārabdhaṁ naiva muñcati I
iti yac chrūyate śāstre tan nirākriyate 'dhunā II 90 II

90. *The theory of the Scripture, according to which the* prārabdha *does not lose its influence on the subject even after knowledge of the* ātman, *is now refuted.*

In these *sūtras* there is the concept of *karma* according to *advaita* metaphysics. Śaṅkara in his *Vivekacūḍāmaṇi* writes:

"It has been objected that, despite the assiduous practice of meditation, perceptions from the external world are received. The *Śruti*, however, maintains that this is the consequence of the *prārabdhakarma*. This can be inferred from evident results."

"The *prārabdha* persists even in the slightest perception of attraction or repulsion; the effect, however, derives from a previous action. [On the other hand] no effect without a cause has ever been seen."

"Realizing 'I am *Brahman*,' the ascetic destroys at once the *saṁcitakarma* accumulated during innumerable *kalpas*, just as actions performed in a dream vanish on waking."

"Being free and indifferent as ether, the ascetic can no longer be touched by *karma* that is yet to mature."

"The *prārabdhakarma* is too powerful for the disciple (*sādhaka*) to restrain; it will exhaust itself with the extinction of its fruits. The other two types of *karma*, that proceeding from previous actions (*saṁcita*) and that whose effects have not yet matured (*āgāmin*), will instead be burnt to ashes in the fire of knowledge. However, none of these three types of *karma* is capable of touching the ascetic who has realized *Brahman* and lives in identity with It."

"For the *muni* [silent ascetic] who lives within his own *ātman* as non-dual *Brahman*, and free from superimpositions (*upādhis*), the question of knowing whether his *prārabdha* exists or not is meaningless.

Does one who wakes up retain even the slightest rapport with the objects of his dream?"[1]

The *Śruti,* in some passages, states that even the *jñānin* is not free from *prārabdhakarma*, and Śaṅkara in the commentaries to the *Chāndogya Upaniṣad* (VI. XIV.2), the *Brahmasūtra* (4.1.15) and the *Bhagavadgīta* (IV.37), shares this thesis of religious order, but in his *Vivekacūḍāmaṇi*, in this work and also elsewhere, he has dealt with the question of *karma* from the truly metaphysical point of view of *Advaita.*

tattvajñānodayād ūrdhvaṁ prārabdhaṁ naiva vidyate I
dehādīnām asattvāt tu yathā svapno vibodhataḥ II 91 II

91. *After knowledge of Reality the* prārabdha *verily ceases to exist because the nonexistence of the body has been recognized. Thus, for one who is awake the reality of the dream is meaningless.*

Karma is consubstantial to the vehicles-bodies. For the *jñānin,* the various sheaths of the *jīva* are nothing but simple modifications of *prakṛti*, devoid of substantial reality; therefore, of what *prārabdha* can one speak regarding the one who has burned *avidyā* in the fire of Knowledge-realization?

karma janmāntarīyaṁ yat prārabdham iti kīrtitam I
tat tu janmāntarābhāvāt puṁso naivāsti karhicit II 92 II

---

[1] Śaṅkara, *Vivekacūḍāmaṇi*, *sūtras* 445-447, 449, 453-454, op. cit.

92. *The* karma *of a preceding life is known as* prārabdha, *but for an entity of knowledge, in the absence of a future life, this* [prārabdha] *truly does not exist.*

svapnadeho yathādhyastas tathaivāyaṁ hi dehakaḥ ।
adhyastasya kuto janma janmābhāve hi tat kutaḥ ॥ 93 ॥

93. *As the body of dream is a superimposition* [*on the dreamer*], *so the* [*waking*] *body is a superimposition* [*on the* ātman]. *So, how can the real birth of a superimposition be possible? And in the absence of birth how can that* [*the* prārabdha] *be?*

The body of the dreamer, although *substantial*, is nothing but a mental modification that vanishes as soon as the individual wakes up. So the body of the waking state is also a modification, "more substantial" and apparently more lasting, of that same operative and molding mind. This body, though, has no reality whatsoever if the fire of Knowledge has been able to dispel it.

There can be *karma* as long as there is identification of the entity with the body, but when the identification ceases, also ceases the existence of the body with its attributes and manifestations.

upādānaṁ prapañcasya mṛdbhāṇḍasyeva kathyate ।
ajñānaṁ caiva vedāntais tasmin naṣṭe kva viśvatā ॥ 94 ॥

94. Vedānta *states that* [*metaphysical*] *ignorance constitutes material cause for the phenomenal world, as clay for a jar. By destroying ignorance, how can that phenomenal world subsist?*

Regarding the *prārabdhakarma* we give the following similitude drawn from the physics of astronomy. Today we can perceive echoes of radio waves of a star that does not exist any longer. Therefore for the star in question the present echo-effect is truly non-existent.

One who has awakened (*jīvanmukta* = liberated during life) does not respond any longer to the inertial, limited echo that is of a certain phenomenal order without life. *Karma* regards the various bodies-sheaths and the *ahaṁkāra*, the "sense of ego." Whoever has placed himself beyond time has placed himself in the eternal present.

yathā rajjuṁ parityajya sarpaṁ gṛhṇāti vai bhramāt ǀ
tadvat satyam avijñāya jagat paśyati mūḍhadhīḥ ǁ 95 ǁ

95. *As an individual in absence of* avidyā *sees only the rope without any snake, so, on the opposite side, an obscured individual sees only the phenomenon-world* [*without underlying reality*].

rajjurūpe parijñāte sarpakhaṇḍaṁ na tiṣṭhati ǀ
adhiṣṭhāne tathā jñāte prapañcaḥ śūnyatāṁ gataḥ ǁ 96 ǁ

96. *As when the real nature of the rope is known the appearance of the snake disappears, so the phenomenon-world disappears completely when its foundation* (adhiṣṭāna) *is realized.*

dehasyāpi prapañcatvāt prārabdhāvasthitiḥ kutaḥ ǀ
ajñānijanabodhārthaṁ prārabdhaṁ vakti vai śrutiḥ ǁ 97 ǁ

97. *Besides, how can the [physical] body, being of the same nature as the phenomenon-world, have the* prārabdhakarma*? If the* Śruti *speaks about it, it is just to [tranquilize] the non-knower* (ajñāna).

The *Śruti* speaks about *prārabdha* only for those who do not yet have Knowledge and who therefore interpret life in terms of phenomenon. So, that reflected echo of sound waves of the star no longer existing is perceivable only by those who are in a determined range of spacial phenomena.

kṣīyante cāsya karmāṇi tasmin dṛṣṭe parāvare I
bahutvaṁ tan niṣedhārthaṁ śrutyā gītaṁ ca yat sphuṭam II 98 II

98. *"When That, Supreme and non-Supreme, has been realized, the knot of the heart is severed, all doubts are dispelled and for him [the effects of all] actions are destroyed." Here the use by the* Śruti *of the plural [actions] is openly declared, and therefore the* prārabdha *is included.*

The quotation of the *Śruti* refers to the *Muṇḍaka Upaniṣad* (II.II.8).

It is evident that this passage of the *Upaniṣad* is in reference to any action (*karma*). The Supreme and the non-Supreme are represented by *Brahman nirguṇa* (without attributes) and by *Brahman saguṇa* (with attributes).

ucyate 'jñair balāc caitat tadānarthadvayāgamaḥ I
vedāntamatahānaṁ ca yato jñānam iti śrutiḥ II 99 II

99. *If the non-knower arbitrarily still maintains this, he not only falls into two absurdities, but runs the risk of straying from the conclusion of* Vedānta. *It is necessary to comprehend the* Śruti *properly in order to have true knowledge.*

With their statements, the supporters of *prārabdha* fall into two absurdities; first: liberation from all duality would be impossible because the reality of the *prārabdha* and the *ātman* would continue to subsist. Second: if Knowledge-realization cannot destroy all possible duality, the same *Śruti,* upon which the supporters of the *prārabdha* also rely, loses its value.

The ultimate conclusions of *Vedānta* demonstrate that only one Reality exists: *Brahman* and all empirical dualities are nothing but the objectified reflections of *māyā.* When in some passages the *Śruti* speaks of duality, it is considering only the empirical point of view, and this in order to let the less-versed ones comprehend.

tripañcāṅgāny atho vakṣye pūrvoktasya hi labdhaye |
taiś ca sarvaiḥ sadā kāryaṁ nididhyāsanam eva tu || 100 ||

100. *Now, to achieve the mentioned* [*Knowledge*], *I will explain fifteen steps that must be continuously practiced and meditated upon.*

The previous *sūtras* demonstrate that we are *Brahman*; from this *sūtra*, instead, are expounded the means to achieve It.

nityābhyāsād ṛte prāptir na bhavet saccidātmanaḥ |
tasmād brahma nididhyāset jijñāsuḥ śreyase ciram || 101 ||

101. *The* ātman, *which is absolute existence* (sat) *and knowledge* (cit), *cannot be realized without constant practice. So the quester must meditate at length on the supreme* Brahman.

In referring to the *ātman*, the *Upaniṣad* defines it in this way:

> "This is the *ātman* indicated as: not this, not this. It is ungraspable because, in truth, it cannot be grasped; indestructible because, in truth, it is not subject to destruction; without contact because, in truth, it has no contact with anything; self-contained because it does not waver or suffer pain."[1]

yamo hi niyamas tyāgo maunaṁ deśaś ca kālatā I
āsanaṁ mūlabandhaś ca dehasāmyaṁ ca dṛksthitiḥ II 102 II

prāṇasaṁyamanaṁ ca eva pratyāhāraś ca dhāraṇā I
ātmadhyānaṁ samādhiś ca proktānyaṅgāni vai kramāt II 103 II

102-103. *These are the steps: mastery of the sensory apparatus* (yama), *control over thoughts* (niyama), *detachment* (tyāga), *silence* (mauna), *space* (deśa) *and time* (kāla), *position* (āsana), *absorption into the root* (mūlabhanda), *corporeal equilibrium* (dehasāmya), *steadiness of vision* (dṛksthiti), *control of the vital energies* (prāṇasaṁyamana), *mental abstraction* (pratyāhāra), *concentration* (dhāraṇā), *meditation on the* ātman (ātmadhyāna), samādhi.

These fifteen steps differ a little from the "eight means" of the *Yoga* of Patañjali.

---

[1] *Bṛhadāraṇyaka Upaniṣad* IV.IV.22.

sarvaṁ brahmeti vijñānād indriya grāmasaṁyamaḥ ǀ
yamo 'yam iti saṁprokto 'bhyasanīyo muhurmuhuḥ ǁ 104 ǁ

104. "Brahman *is all"; from this knowledge insistently realized [stems] the mastering of the sensory apparatus. This is rightly called* yama [*first step*].

In the *Māṇḍūkya Upaniṣad* (I) it is said:

"*Om* is all this. A clear explanation of this: what is past, present and future is only the *oṁkāra*. And what is beyond this threefold temporality is still the syllable *Om*."

Śaṅkara comments: "...In the same manner as a thing is known with the name that belongs to it, so the supreme *Brahman* cannot be known but through his name: *Om*. This supreme *Brahman* is, really, *Om*.

"The present chapter offers the explanation of That, i.e., *Om*, as supreme *Brahman* and non-supreme *Brahman*."

In the *Yogasūtra* of Patañjali, *yama*, which is the first of the eight (*aṅgas*), is defined as: prohibition, self-control and moral restraint.

> "The prohibitions are: non-violence (*ahiṃsā*), non-falsity (*satya*), non-appropriation (*asteya*), continence (*brahmacarya*), non-possessiveness (*aparigraha*)."[1]

For the disciple *jñānin*, on the other hand, mastery of the senses is achieved with the burning aspiration toward the comprehension that *Brahman* is all-pervading and represents the Totality.

---

[1] Patañjali, *The Regal Way to Realization (Yogadarśana)*, II.30, op. cit.

The momentum toward *vidyā* (knowledge) re-orients one's entire sensory energetic world. It is this re-orientation toward our inner that extinguishes every extroverted movement of appropriation of any order or degree.

Truth unveils to those who are capable of loving it, and in that love for truth the senses find their right direction.

sajātīyapravāhaś ca vijātīyatiraskṛtiḥ ।
niyamo hi parānando niyamāt kriyate budhaiḥ ॥ 105 ॥

105. *Being constantly on a single thought content, to the exclusion of all other thoughts, is called* niyama. *What represents supreme beatitude is regularly practiced by the sage [second step].*

The second *aṅga* of the *Yogasūtra*, *nyama*, is conceived in this way:

> "The observances (*niyama*) are: purity [inner and outer], being content, burning aspiration, study and abandon to *Īśvara*."[1]

For the *jñānin*, *niyama* consists in directing thought to the single and fundamental content of reflection: "*Brahman* is all" and "I [as *jīva*] am *Brahman*."

This absorption of the mind into *Brahman* resolves all duality, cause of conflict; thus consciousness finds itself again in its essential condition, outside of any illusory content. The control of the mind is obtained, therefore, in exercising thought to find oneself as brahmanic Unity.

---

[1] Ibid. II.32.

tyāgaḥ prapañcarūpasya cidātmatvāvalokanāt I
tyāgo hi mahatāṁ pūjyaḥ sadyo mokṣamayo yataḥ II 106 II

106. *Consciously realizing the* ātman, *one arrives at detachment from the phenomenal universe. This constitutes the true renunciation of the Sage, because it leads to instant Liberation* [*third step*].

When knowledge-consciousness, after intuitive discernment, discovers the rope (the *ātman* in our case), the illusory snake (mistaken for the rope) vanishes, whereby detachment acquires a factual basis. We are attached to objects because we believe them to be real and capable of giving total fulfillment. We anxiously run after the snake, which escapes us continuously because it represents a simple process, becoming, phenomenon.

This senseless wandering in the realm of *saṁsāra* forces us to construct a surrogate world capable of satisfying our incompleteness, but such satisfaction can only resolve into bewilderment because compensating does not lead to true joy without object.

Patañjali defines detachment or non-attachment (*vairāgya*) in this way:

> "Non-attachment is conscious mastery on the part of that one who has ceased thirsting for visible and audible [revealed] objects."

"That supreme [detachment] is represented [also] by the total freedom from the *guṇas* as the result of awareness of the *puruśa*."[1]

This last *sūtra* offers *paravairāgya* (supreme detachment).

yasmād vāco nivartante aprāpya manasā saha |
yan maunaṁ yogibhir gamyaṁ tad bhavet sarvadā budhaḥ || 107 ||

107. *The Sage must always be one with that [all-encompassing] Silence* (mauna) *in front of which words and thoughts recede onto themselves without reaching it. Only the* yogi *can achieve it [fourth step]*.

Silence is the symbol of the *ātman* because it remains out of manifestation-movement whereby it does not need any action or discursiveness.

In the *Upaniṣad* we read:

"One who has realized the fullness of *Brahman*, whence words recede together with thought, unable to reap it, has nothing more to fear."[2]

vāco yasmān nivartante tad vaktuṁ kena śakyate |
prapañco yadi vaktavyaḥ so 'pi śabdavivarjitaḥ || 108 ||

108. *That [Silence] whence words recede. Even the description of the phenomenal world escapes words.*

---

[1] Ibid. I.15-16.

[2] *Taittirīya Upaniṣad* II.IX.1.

iti vā tad bhaven maunaṁ satāṁ sahajasaṁjñitaṁ |
girā maunaṁ tu bālānāṁ prayuktaṁ brahmavādibhiḥ || 109 ||

109. *Thus that Silence [the inexpressibility of* Brahman *and the world] can also be defined by the Sages as congenital silence. But, silence is imposed on children by the Masters of* Brahman.

Both *Brahman* and phenomenal *appearance* (*māyā*) cannot be described and catalogued because the former, constituting the Absolute, cannot be the object of empirical knowledge, and the latter, as soon as it is considered, has already vanished. We can say that that one who truly comprehends puts himself in the psychological position of the "sphinx," while the non-knower tries to speak of that which, after all, he *is* not; rather, he is forced to speak precisely because he has not comprehended.

"The *Tao* that can be named *Tao*
Is not the eternal *Tao*.
The Name that can be named
Is not the eternal Name."[1]

The true attitude toward Knowledge-realization (*vidyā*) is that of silent absorption into truth, rather than continuous conceptualization in order to satisfy the nature of the notional mind.

For this reason all traditional works are synthetic and symbolic; in this way one is forced to work more with supraconscious intuition than with the analytical mind, which is of the ego order (*ahaṁkāra*).

---

[1] Lao-Tze, *Tao-Tê-Ching* 1.

ādāv ante ca madhye ca jano yasmin na vidyate ǀ
yenedaṁ satataṁ vyāptaṁ sa deśo vijanaḥ smṛtaḥ ǁ 110 ǁ

110. *That solitude is known as all-pervading space [ether] in which every thing does not exist in the beginning, in the middle or in the end [fifth step].*

kalanāt sarvabhūtānāṁ brahmādīnāṁ nimeṣataḥ ǀ
kālaśabdena nirdiṣṭo hy akhaṇḍānandako 'dvayaḥ ǁ 111 ǁ

111. *The One-without-a-second* [Brahman], *which is undivided fullness, is indicated by the word time because with a flash of its glance it makes appear* Brahmā *with all the beings [sixth step].*

Brahmā (the One as principial cause of all that is, the first superimposition) and all the *jīvas* appear, through the magic of *māyā*, not in a temporal succession, but simultaneously as happens in dream when suddenly the nocturnal universe appears in its composite totality.

Time and space are nothing but becoming itself; they are process and change considered from the point of view of the empirical mind. As the mind progressively resolves itself, time-space fades until it completely disappears; then the "ever present" takes the place of the fragmentary, of the succession or evolution and becoming. We can say that time and space contract until they annul themselves.

sukhenaiva bhaved yasminn ajasraṁ brahmacintanam ǀ
āsanaṁ tadvijānīyān netarat sukhanāśanam ǁ 112 ǁ

112. *We must know the right position through which meditation on* Brahman *happens spontaneously and incessantly and not that which could push away one's serenity* [*seventh step*].

Patañjali speaks in this way about the "position" of the body:

"The position [must be] steady and comfortable."[1]

After all, for both the *Rāja Yoga* of Patañjali and *Vedānta*, the technique of the "position" is directed toward the elimination of any source of mental disturbance. In other words, it is a particular psychological attitude that is engaged automatically if the mind is attentive to the seed of meditation.

Whenever we try to meditate, many subconscious or corporeal stimuli arise as interferences and distractions; it is necessary not to be concerned with these stimuli and to bring, instead, the attention on the object of meditation, with simplicity, innocence and without dramatizing.

siddhaṁ yat sarvabhūtādi viśvādhiṣṭhānam avyayam I
yasmin siddhāḥ samāviṣṭās tad vai siddhāsanaṁ viduḥ II 113 II

113. *The Immutable is known as the root of all the entities and the support of the entire universe, and the enlightened is completely absorbed into it; this* [*attitude*] *is known as* siddhāsana [*eighth step*].

---

[1] Patañjali, *The Regal Way to Realization (Yogadarśana)*, II.46, op. cit.

Siddhāsana is a particular *yoga* position, as is the other one called *padmāsana*; but in our context it refers to an attitude or "mental position."

True *siddhāsana* is realized when the mind is brought back to the root of all things, when, eliminating all superimpositions on the real, it sinks and lets itself be absorbed by what we are.

yan mūlaṁ sarvabhūtānāṁ yan mūlaṁ cittabandhanam ।
mūlabandhaḥ sadā sevyo yogyo 'sau rājayoginām ॥ 114 ॥

114. *What constitutes the origin of all existence-appearance and that resolves the mind is known, precisely, as the resolving root [of the mind] and [this attitude] should always be adopted by the* rājayogis.

The mind, cause of continuous and conflictual projections, can be slowed and resolved only if one discovers the reality underlying it.

aṅgānāṁ samatāṁ vidyāt same brahmaṇi līnatām ।
no cen naiva samānatvam ṛjutvaṁ śuṣkavṛkṣavat ॥ 115 ॥

115. *Absorption into the homogeneous* Brahman *is known as the equilibrium of the body, while the simple straightness [of the body] is similar to an unbalanced dry tree [ninth step].*

When there is absorption of the consciousness-mind into *Brahman*, the body finds itself in a perfect and natural state of equilibrium, whereas if one dwells with the will on simple corporeal equilibrium, a clumsy and unnatural position results.

When consciousness is put at the *center* of the axis, harmony prevails, manifesting itself everywhere.

dṛṣṭiṁ jñānamayīṁ kṛtvā paśyed brahmamayaṁ jagat |
sā dṛṣṭiḥ paramodārā na nāsāgrāvalokinī || 116 ||

116. *Sublime vision of knowledge is to consider the world supported* (māyā) *by* Brahman *itself and not to maintain that the tip of the nose must be observed* [*tenth step*].

There are certain *Haṭhayoga* exercises that consist in concentrating on the tip of the nose, the tongue, etc. Although not at all banal because they conceal the acquisition of certain psychic powers, nonetheless for the *jñānin*, who aims at the realization of Identity with the ultimate Reality, what matters is to correct the erroneous vision of the world; in other words, to resolve *avidyā*, cause of prison in the three levels of gross, subtle and germinal-causal.

draṣṭṛ darśanadṛśyānāṁ virāmo yatra vā bhavet |
dṛṣṭis tatraiva kartavyā na nāsāgrāvalokinī || 117 ||

117. *Or, have the vision only of That in which ceases the distinctions of seer, seen and seeing and not* [*of concentrating*] *on the tip of the nose.*

In the preceding *sūtra* there is meditation on *saguṇa Brahman* (with attributes: the first superimposition on the absolute *Brahman*), while in this one the accent is put on *nirguṇa Brahman*, the One-without-a-second unqualified, in which all ideas of perceiver, perception and perceived disappear.

cittādisarvabhāveṣu brahmatvenaiva bhāvanāt ।
nirodhaḥ sarvavṛttīnāṁ prāṇāyāmaḥ sa ucyate ॥ 118 ॥

118. *The suspension of all modifications of the mind, with respect to the various mental states as* citta, *etc., happens only in* [*realizing*] Brahman. *This is* prāṇāyāma [*eleventh step*].

In *Haṭhayoga*, *prāṇāyāma* consists in suspension of the breath, while in *Jñānayoga* the suspension of the pranic-physical breath corresponds to apprehending *Brahman*.

In the first case there is a kind of *samādhi* in which the consciousness-mind exits the body to find itself on other planes; in the second there is a *samādhi*-realization "with open eyes," whereby in every dimension—gross, subtle or informal—one can "see" *Brahman* and only *Brahman*.

In other words, some *yogis* can only find peace of the heart in the subtle or causal states by absorbing themselves in an object of meditation, while the *jñānin* finds it at all levels, including those of a gross order, because *Brahman* is not here or there, but is the substratum, or foundation, which persists and does not depend on place and time.

niṣedhanaṁ prapañcasya recakākhyaḥ samīraṇaḥ ।
brahmaivāsmīti yā vṛttiḥ pūrako vāyur īritaḥ ॥ 119 ॥

119. *The solution of the world of names and forms is known as* recaka (*exhalation*); *the recognition "I am* Brahman" *is called* pūraka (*inhalation*).

tatas tadvṛttinaiścalyaṁ kuṁbhakaḥ prāṇasaṁyamaḥ ।
ayaṁ cāpi prabuddhānāṁ ajñānāṁ ghrāṇapīḍanam ॥ 120 ॥

120. *And the constant absorption in that recognition is called* kumbhaka (*retention of the breath*). *This is the real control of the vital force* (prāṇāyāma) *of the enlightened; the profane tortures his nose instead.*

This way of considering *prāṇāyāma* on the part of the *jñānin* is interesting. To realize the ascesis, he starts from the buddhic vehicle, and the *sattva-buddhi* constitutes the supraconscious intellective intuition, the immediate discernment, the pure intelligence (*cit*). Using discernment, the *jñānin* "comprehends" the ultimate Reality, and thereby he resolves into it.

This is precisely the metaphysical path, consisting in continuous integrations and recognitions of *Brahman*. One pursuing it is presumed to have already applied a certain discipline of the will and to have reoriented the emotional-subtle vehicle. His love toward *vidyā* (knowledge) must lead him always further on the planes of universal vision, despite the events of the profane life.

The way of the *jñānin* is that of defeating *avidyā-māyā*, ignorance about the nature of Reality, and not that of finding sensory fulfillment with some power of any order or degree, nor psychological quiet because one is not yet able to stand on one's own feet by oneself.

One who does not know how to *fly*, and thus to leave any psychophysical stand-support, would be well-advised to turn to those types of *Yoga* that primarily aim at harmonizing the psychophysical nature through devotion to the divine Ideal. The *advaita* path is a "Way of Fire" and some might get burned because they are not ready.[1]

For the classical *prāṇāyāma* refer to the commentary to *sūtra* 27 of chapter V of the *Bhagavadgītā*.[2]

viṣayeṣv ātmatāṁ dṛṣṭvā manasaś citi majjanam I
pratyāhāraḥ sa vijñeyo 'bhyasanīyo mumukṣubhiḥ II 121 II

121. *The abstraction of the mind from all objects and the absorption in the vision* (dṛṣṭi) *of the* ātmā *are known as* pratyāhāra *by the researcher of Liberation* [*twelfth step*].

In the *Yogasūtra* we read:

"There is *pratyāhāra* when the senses are no longer in contact with the respective objects, assuming [thus]

---

[1] For the various types of *Yoga*, see Raphael, *Essence and Purpose of Yoga: The Initiatory Pathways to the Transcendent*, in particular the chapters "Jñāna-yoga" and "Asparśa-yoga" (Shaftesbury, Dorset: Element Books, 1996); for the "Path of Fire," see the chapter "Colorless Fire" in Raphael, *The Threefold Pathway of Fire: Thoughts that Vibrate* (New York: Aurea Vidyā, 2000).

[2] cf. *Bhagavadgītā: The Celestial Song*, translation from the Sanskrit and commentary by Raphael (New York: Aurea Vidyā, 2012).

identity with the mind's own nature [which remains steady and colorless]."[1]

So, the absorption of the sensory *manas* into the supreme Intelligence (*cit*) makes every form-object vanish precisely because the latter is projected from the mind. At a psychological level, when we are absorbed in a particular problem, we remain completely abstracted from any type of external perception. This implies intensely focalizing on a datum so as to remain isolated from all the pressures and stimuli that can come from our subconscious or the surrounding world.

yatra yatra mano yāti brahmaṇas tatra darśanāt |
manaso dhāraṇaṁ caiva dhāraṇā sā parā matā || 122 ||

122. *The stability of the mind on* Brahman [*alone*], *starting from any object whatsoever, is known as* dhāraṇā [*thirteenth step*].

In the *Yogasūtra* it is written:

"Concentration (*dhāraṇā*) is fixing the *citta* on one point."[2]

Therefore, for the *jñānin* it is a question of focalizing the attention on the ultimate Reality of the datum, transcending, thus, the formal and nominal aspects.

---

[1] Patañjali, *The Regal Way to Realization (Yogadarśana)*, II.54, op. cit.

[2] Ibid. III.1.

brahmaivāsmīti sadvṛttyā nirālambatayā sthitiḥ ।
dhyānaśabdena vikhyātā paramānandadāyinī ॥ 123 ॥

123. *When one remains independent from everything following the persistent recognition "I am* Brahman" *there is* dhyāna, *which produces supreme happiness* [*fourteenth step*].

Patañjali states:

"Fixing oneself uninterruptedly on such point is meditation (*dhyāna*)."[1]

But the mind finds its effective consummation when it is absorbed by Identity with *That*. Therefore, also when it is in meditation on a suprasensible datum it still is not perfectly resolved.

nirvikāratayā vṛttyā brahmākāratayā punaḥ ।
vṛttivismaraṇaṁ samyak samādhir jñānasaṁjñakaḥ ॥ 124 ॥

124. *Complete transcendence of every mental activity, because identity with* Brahman *has been attained, is considered* samādhi *or Knowledge* [*fifteenth step*].

Patañjali in the *Yogasūtra* maintains:

"The same [meditation], when it takes only the essential form of the object and not that of its mental representation, is called *samādhi*."

"The three [applied] to a single object [form] *saṁyama*."

[1] Ibid. III.2.

"Mastering it [one achieves] the light of knowledge."[1]

It is necessary to consider that *samādhi* is neither a "trance," as is generally thought, nor any passive condition whatsoever of the consciousness. *Samādhi* is the apex of an active and supraconscious awareness, constituting a state of "immediate recognition" of reality as self-unveiled.

Samādhi unveils the intimate truth of things; therefore it relates to the archetypes and moves on the plane of the archetypes. It is not, beware, intellective intuition, which concerns a subordinate position and represents the "descent" into the three-dimensional mind of an archetypal truth.

Samādhi constitutes the direct contemplation of the archetype; and, at certain levels, the archetype is born from the Being itself. When the *eye* of *samādhi* is open, we do not need the mind to discriminate and deduce, because it unveils the essential knowledge.

For the *jñānin*, *samādhi* is Knowledge-realization, and this can be achieved on all levels of Being because if *Brahman* is the foundation of all, then in any time-space one can see *Brahman* and in any time-space one can "be" *Brahman*.

imañ cākṛtrim ānandaṁ tāvat sādhu samabhyaset |
vaśyo yāvat kṣaṇāt puṁsaḥ prayuktaḥ san bhavet svayam || 125 ||

---

[1] Ibid. III.3-5.

125. [*The* yogi] *should accurately practice the steps that unveil natural beatitude until this becomes a spontaneous expression in his life.*

tataḥ sādhananirmuktaḥ siddho bhavati yogirāṭ ।
tatsvarūpaṁ na caitasya viṣayo manaso girām ॥ 126 ॥

126. *Thus one, best among* yogis, *having attained perfection, is freed of all practice. The real nature of such a* yogi *can never be the object of mental representation or of words.*

When one is "completeness," every means, exercise, *sādhanā*, etc., is exhausted because the aim has been achieved. The very Scriptures have fulfilled their purpose and the being finds itself *jīvanmukta*, i.e., beyond any verbal-conceptual framework.

"One who has realized the fullness of *Brahman*, from which words recede together with thought, unable to reap it, has nothing more to fear."[1]

The "Way of Fire" ends for lack of fuel. So, to say it with Plato, one has arrived at "the end of the journey."

samādhau kriyamāṇe tu vighnāny āyānti vai balāt ।
anusandhānarāhityam ālasyaṁ bhogalālasam ॥ 127 ॥

127. *In the practice of* samādhi *certain obstacles may appear, such as a lack of research, laziness or sensory pleasures,*

---

[1] *Taittirīya Upaniṣad* II.IX.1.

layas tamaś ca vikṣepo rasāsvādaś ca śūnyatā |
evaṁ yad vighnabāhulyaṁ tyājyaṁ brahmavidā śanaiḥ ||128 ||

128. *torpor, distraction, taste of happiness, confusion and obtuseness. When, though, one aspires to the Knowledge of* Brahman, *gradually one frees oneself from such obstacles.*

During the ascesis, because of inevitable psychophysical conflicts, certain movements of the consciousness can manifest, which seemingly could be mistaken for spiritual progress. Mental torpor, for instance, which may emerge in some phases when retreating into the *center*, may be considered as an advancement, while in effect it is not. One may have "psychic powers," pleasurable feelings like a sensory happiness or enhanced vital abilities, but these states also are aleatory and do not represent the ultimate aim; therefore, they should be transcended.

bhāvavṛttyā hi bhāvatvaṁ śūnyavṛttyā hi śūnyatā |
brahmavṛttyā hi pūrṇatvaṁ tathā pūrṇatvam abhyaset || 129 ||

129. *When the individual thinks of an object, he becomes that object; when he thinks of the void* (ākāśa), *he becomes that void, while if he concentrates on* Brahman, *he attains perfection. Therefore one must constantly think of perfection.*

The *Upaniṣad* states:

"One becomes what one thinks. This is the eternal mystery."[1]

---

[1] *Maitry Upaniṣad* VI.34.3.

If the individual constantly thinks about unhappiness, sooner or later he will be unhappiness; if he thinks about evil, he will be instrument of evil; if he thinks about violence, he will be instrument of violence; if he thinks about universal Love, he will be instrument of all-pervading Love.

The individual reaps what he sows with his own thoughts, which are truly substantial and dynamic *entities*.

This *sūtra* is very important because it unveils the secret of the right mental action.

ye hi vṛttiṁ jahatyenaṁ brahmākhyāṁ pāvaniṁ parām ।
vṛthaiva te tu jīvanti paśubhiś ca samā narāḥ ॥ 130 ॥

130. *Those who do not bring their mind on* Brahman, *supremely purifying, live uselessly and can consider themselves at the same level as lower entities.*

The aim of the human being is to find itself in perfect consciousness. One who strays from this purpose, even if he accomplishes interesting things, fails the dictates of his own nature.

There is no higher action or education than that leading to the rediscovery of oneself. There is no higher purpose or divine plan than that pushing to unveil what we really are.

"Considerate la vostra semenza:
fatti non foste a viver come bruti,
ma per seguir virtute e conoscenza."[1]

---

[1] Dante, *Inferno* XXVI.118. "Consider your origin: you were not made to live like brutes, but to pursue virtue and knowledge."

ye hi vṛttiṁ vijānanti jñātvāpi vardhayanti ye ।
te vai satpuruṣā dhanyā vandhyāste bhuvanatraye ॥ 131 ॥

131. *Blessed are those who, having [acquired] it, develop ever more the awareness [of* Brahman]. *They are respected in the three worlds.*

Intuitive knowledge and that of *samādhi* of *Brahma* must become consciousness until there is Identity with *That.* When this has been realized, one is beyond humans and gods.

yeṣāṁ vṛttiḥ samā vṛddhā paripakvā ca sā punaḥ ।
te vai sadbrahmatāṁ prāptā netare śabdavādināḥ ॥ 132 ॥

132. *Only those whose growth has been matured and [remains] always present [can be] in identity with the ever-existent* Brahman, *and not those who simply talk about it.*

The paradox is that all want to be free, but prefer the freedom of the *empirical I*, or ego, which is contingent and conflictual, and not the Freedom *from* the ego, which takes us to the "end of the journey" and therefore to the end of every type of conflict and travail.

kuśalā brahmavārtāyāṁ vṛttihīnāḥ surāgiṇaḥ ।
te 'py ajñānatayā nūnaṁ punar āyānti yānti ca ॥ 133 ॥

133. *Also those who speak about* Brahman *in a competent way, but have no realization and are attached [to the world of names and forms], because of their ignorance, they repeatedly come and go.*

In order to avoid considering *Vedānta* a simple speculative philosophy or *Brahman* itself to be a mental abstraction, it would be well to reflect on these *sūtras.*

nimeṣārdhaṁ na tiṣṭhanti vṛttiṁ brahmamayīṁ vinā ǀ
yathā tiṣṭhanti brahmādyāḥ sanakādyāḥ śukādayaḥ ǁ 134 ǁ

134. [*The true* yogis], *instead, at every instant are permeated with the thought of* Brahman, *precisely as* Brahmā, Sanaka, Śuka *and others.*

kārye kāraṇatāyātā kāraṇe na hi kāryatā ǀ
kāraṇatvaṁ tato gacchet kāryābhāve vicārataḥ ǁ 135 ǁ

135. *The cause is such because it inheres in the effect and not vice versa; hence we can infer that lacking the effect, the cause also disappears.*

Cause and effect are correlated terms because where there is a cause there is also an effect and where there is an effect there is also a cause. Now, lacking the cause, the effect cannot subsist, and lacking the effect, the cause, as such, cannot be posited because there is no reference that can indicate a cause.

Until we admit to the hierarchy of cause and effects, we stay in the domain of *māyā*. It is necessary to comprehend that cause and effect do not constitute anything but superimpositions on the Real-absolute and that these superimpositions must be eliminated.

atha śuddhaṁ bhaved vastu yad vai vācām agocaram ǀ
draṣṭavyaṁ mṛdghaṭenaiva dṛṣṭāntena punaḥ punaḥ ǁ 136 ǁ

136. [*So*] *remains that single and pure Reality* [Brahman-*without-a-second*] *that is beyond mental categories. This can be truly comprehended with the example of the clay and the vase.*

"My dear, from a single piece of clay all what is made of clay is known, while all its modifications are nothing but mere denomination of name, whereby the only reality is the clay."[1]

Such an analogy refers to *Brahman saguṇa*, i.e., to the principial Cause that contains all the archetype-ideas of the entire manifestation. In turn, this principial Cause (ontological state) finds its own raison d'être in *Brahman nirguṇa,* which represents the substratum or the foundation by which all can be and exist in its own unity and harmony.

anenaiva prakāreṇa vṛttir brahmātmikā bhavet I
udeti śuddhacittānāṁ vṛttijñānaṁ tataḥ param II 137 II

137. *Only in this way is born the pure awareness that determines re-absorption into* Brahman.

Through discerning between real and non-real one arrives at the conclusion that only *Brahman* is the imperishable *constant*, devoid of modifications and duality. See also *sūtra* VII of the *Māṇḍukya Upaniṣad* and the related *kārikā* of Gauḍapāda.

[1] *Chāndogya Upaniṣad* VI.I.4.

kāraṇaṁ vyatirekeṇa pumān ādau vilokayet ǀ
anvayena punas tad dhi kārye nityaṁ prapaśyati ǁ 138 ǁ

138. *Before everything else, one must examine the cause with the negative method followed by the positive method, because it always inheres in the effect.*

Every cause can be deduced by a positive or negative assertion. An example of the first case is: "where there is an effect there must be a cause"; and an example of the second case is: "where there is no cause there is no effect."

kārye hi kāraṇaṁ paśyet paścāt kāryaṁ visarjayet ǀ
kāraṇatvaṁ tato gacched avaśiṣṭaṁ bhavet muniḥ ǁ 139 ǁ

139. *One must consider the effect in the cause, and then resolve the cause. What remains the Sage realizes.*

From an empirical point of view, the effect is nothing but the cause having manifested a certain determination. When the cause, as such, produces modifications, disappears or resolves itself, nothing remains but the silent Witness in the pure state. We have seen that cause-effect and time-space respond to *māyā*, movement, change and becoming.

The primordial cause is *Brahman saguṇa*, which represents, as we know, the principial state, the first note-sound, while its indefinite harmonics symbolize the various entities of all orders and degrees.

bhāvitaṁ tīvravegena yad vastu niścayātmanā ǀ
pumāṁs tad dhi bhaveḥ chıghraṁ jñeyaṁ bhramarakıṭavat ǁ 140 ǁ

140. *That one who meditates on something with great assiduity and firm conviction resolves himself in that thing. This may be comprehended with the example of the wasp and the insect.*

A popular belief tells of a wasp capturing an insect, who, thinking constantly about its assailant, transformed itself into a wasp.

adṛśyaṁ bhāvarūpaṁ ca sarvam eva cidātmakam I
sāvadhānatayā nityaṁ svātmānaṁ bhāvayed budhaḥ II 141 II

141. *The Sage must consider with great care the visible, the invisible subtle and everything else as his own* ātman.

dṛśyaṁ hy adṛśyatāṁ nītvā brahmākāreṇa cintayet I
vidvān nityasukhe tiṣṭhed dhiyā cidrasapūrṇayā II 142 II

142. *Having resolved the visible [gross] into the invisible subtle, the Sage considers everything as the* Brahman-*without-a-second.*

ebhir aṅgaiḥ samāyukte rājayoga udāhṛtaḥ I
kiñcit pakvakaṣāyāṇāṁ haṭhayogena saṁyutaḥ II 143 II

143. *Thus [vedāntic]* Rājayoga *has been described. At this point* Haṭhayoga *can be added for those whose mundane desires are extinct only in part.*

Rājayoga, which Śaṅkara speaks of, having a psychological as well as a philosophical nature, may be found difficult for those who have not dominated certain typically physical tendencies or qualities; therefore, *Haṭhayoga* may prove, for them, initially useful.

> paripakvaṁ mano yeṣāṁ kevalo ’yaṁ ca siddhidaḥ ।
> gurudaivatabhaktānāṁ sarveṣāṁ sulabho javāt ॥ 144 ॥

144. *For those whose mind is purified, only this* yoga *is producer of perfection. Purity of mind, also, is accessible to those who are devoted to the Instructor and the Divinity.*

APPENDIX

Knowledge and Ritual Action

Since *Aparokṣānubhūti* is based on *jñāna* Realization, and therefore on Knowledge in its Traditional sense, it was considered helpful to insert this Appendix with Śaṅkara's Introduction to the *Śvetāśvatara Upaniṣad* as it fosters the *jñānin* disciple's correct consciential position.

List of Abbreviations

A.	*Adhyātma Upaniṣad*
Ā.	*Āruṇeya Upaniṣad*
Ai.	*Aitareya Upaniṣad*
Ai. Ā.	*Aitareyāraṇyaka*
Amṛ.	*Amṛtabindu Upaniṣad*
A. Rā.	*Adhyātma Rāmāyaṇa*
Āśra.	*Āśrama Upaniṣad*
Atha.	*Atharvaśira Upaniṣad*
Bha. Gī.	*Bhagavadgītā*
Bṛ.	*Bṛhadāraṇyaka Upaniṣad*
Bra. Pu.	*Brahma Purāṇa*
Bra. Sū.	*Brahmasūtra*
Chā.	*Chāndogya Upaniṣad*
Ī.	*Īśa Upaniṣad or Īśāvāsya Upaniṣad*
Ka.	*Kaṭha Upaniṣad*
Kai.	*Kaivalya Upaniṣad*
Kau.	*Kauṣītakī Upaniṣad*
Kau. Brā.	*Kauṣītakī Brāhmaṇa*
Ke.	*Kena Upaniṣad*
Li. Pu Dhyā	*Liṅgapurāṇa: Dhyānayajñamāhātmyam*
Li. Pu Kā	*Liṅgapurāṇa: Kālakūṭopavyākhyānam*

Mā.	*Māṇḍūkya Upaniṣad*
Ma Bhā. A.	*Mahābhārata, Anuśānaparvan*
Ma Bhā. Ā.	*Mahābhārata, Āśvamedhikaparvan*
Ma Bhā. Śā.	*Mahābhārata, Śāntiparvan*
Ma. Bhā. U.	*Mahābhārata, Udyogaparvam*
Mai.	*Maitrey Upaniṣad*
Mā. Kā.	*Māṇḍūkyakārikā of Gauḍapāda*
Ma. Nā.	*Mahānārāyaṇa Upaniṣad*
Mu.	*Muṇḍaka Upaniṣad*
Nā.	*Nārāyaṇadīpikā*
Nṛ.	*Nṛsiṁhapūrvatāpanyupaniṣad*
Pa.	*Paramahaṁsa Upaniṣad*
Pā. Sū.	*Pāṇini Sūtra*
Pra.	*Praśna Upaniṣad*
Ṛ.	*Ṛgveda*
Śa.	*Śaṅkarānandadīpikā*
Śā.	*Śāṇḍily Upaniṣad*
Śa. Brā.	*Śatapatha Brāhmaṇa*
Śrī. Bhā. Pu.	*Śrīmad Bhāgavata Purāṇa*
Sub.	*Subāla Upaniṣad*
Śu. Ya.	*Śukla Yajurveda*
Śu. Ya. U. Nā.	*Śukla Yajurveda Uttaranārāyaṇam*
Śve.	*Śvetāśvatara Upaniṣad*
Tai.	*Taittirīya Upaniṣad*
Tai. Ā.	*Taittirīya Āraṇyaka*
Tai. Brā.	*Taittirīya Brāhmaṇa*
Tai. Saṁ.	*Taittirīya Saṁhitā*

Vi. Pu.	*Viṣṇu Purāṇa*
Yā. Ya.	*Yājñavalkyayatidharmaśāstra*
Yo.	*Yogaśikha Upaniṣad*
Yo. Vā.	*Yogavāsiṣṭha*

Śaṅkara's Introduction to the Śvetāśvatara Upaniṣad

This brief text, which constitutes a concise introduction to the *Śvetāśvatara Upaniṣad*, has been composed to ease comprehension for those who aspire to Knowledge of *Brahman*.

Although the *ātman* [in its aspect-reflection of *jīva*] is by its own nature *Brahman*, which is [absolute] Consciousness, Being and Fullness, and is non-dual, when it turns to goals of the human order, it is totally limited by innate ignorance—[that ignorance] that resides in oneself, concerns oneself, is perceptible through one's own experience and is intimately associated with that reflection [of the *ātman* which is the *jīva*]—and thus becomes prey of indefinite tribulations; at the same time, because of the same means produced by that ignorance, the *jīva* believes that the end of human existence consists in obtaining the objects of desire, whereas the goal of human existence is not that at all.

Therefore, overcome by attachment and the other [passions] similar to sharks, etc., it misses the goal of liberation, and after having wandered for innumerable and diverse existences, taking the corporeal aspect of gods, humans or animals, etc., it can, thanks to some meritorious action, obtain a birth as *brāhmaṇa* or other [human being] in a suitable condition [for the knowledge of *Brahman*]. Then, when he performs an action, he offers its result to the Lord and frees himself from attachment and from all the other defects. Having attained, therefore, detachment from objects of fruition that belong to this or the other world, thanks to the hatching of the consciousness regarding their impermanent nature, he approaches a Master. So, through the hearing, etc. [the reflection and the deep meditation] of *Vedānta* [made possible] by the Master, he realizes the identity of the *ātman* with *Brahman*: "I [as *jīva*] am *Brahman*," liberating himself from *avidyā* and freeing himself from any pain engendered by it. Because liberation, which consists in the ceasing of the ignorance, is achieved only thanks to the knowledge, it is right that, to this end [that is, that of teaching the knowledge of *Brahman*], the *Upaniṣad* should begin.

That the knowledge of such [identity of the *ātman* with *Brahman*] grants immortality is thus learned from the following passages of the *Śruti* and of the *Smṛti*. [For the *Śruti*, there are the following passages:] "One who realizes It as such becomes immortal here [in this body]" (*Nṛ*. 1.6, *Tai. Ā*. VI.1.6), "No other way exists to lead us" (*Śve*. III.8, VI.15, *Śu. Ya. U. Nā*. 31.17), "...if [it] is not realized here, there is a great ruin" (*Ke*. II.5), "Those who realized That become immortal..." (*Bṛ*. IV.IV.14), "... thus, desiring what and by whose will would one bear the affliction of the body?" (*Bṛ*. IV.IV.12), "Having realized that [splendor that is the *ātman*], one no longer is touched by unworthy action" (*Bṛ*. IV.IV.23), "...the knower of the *ātman* goes beyond suffering" (*Chā*. VII.I.3),

"Realizing That...one escapes from the jaws of death" (*Ka*. I.III.15), "He who knows this supremely immortal *Brahman* as resting in the cave [of the heart], he right here severs the knot of ignorance, my dear" (*Mu*. II.I.10), "The knot of the heart is severed, all doubts dissipate, and for him [the effects of all] acts are destroyed when That, supreme and non-supreme, has been realized" (*Mu*. II.II.8), "As the flowing rivers arrive into the peace of the sea, losing name and form, so the sage, free from name and form, realizes the self-resplendent *Puruṣa*, which transcends even the supreme [undestructible, *avyakta*]" (*Mu*. III.II.8), "Certainly, he who, in truth, knows that supreme *Brahman*, becomes *Brahman* itself" (*Mu*. III. II.9), "He who realizes the same supreme Immutable, in truth, knows That which is without shadow, without body, without the color red, resplendent and without change; in truth, my dear, that one becomes omniscient and the totality itself" (*Pra*. IV.10), "One has to realize That which is worthy of being realized...so that death can no longer afflict you" (*Pra*. VI.6), "...what agitation, what affliction [can there be] for one who recognizes oneself as [supreme] unity?" (*Ī*. 7), "...one achieves immortality through knowledge" (*Ī*. 11), "Having recognized [*Brahman*] in every element [of the threefold world], the resolute sages, leaving this world, become immortal" (*Ke*. II.5), "...having removed the error, one is firmly grounded in the infinite, beatific and supreme world" (*Ke*. IV.9), "...saturated with That, in truth they became immortal" (*Śve*. V.6), "...the incarnated being, merely intuiting that same reality that is the *ātman*, becomes one, perfectly accomplished and free from pain" (*Śve*. II.14), "Those who have realized That achieve immortality..." (*Bṛ.* IV.IV.14), "Knowing that Deva...they achieve immortality" (*Śve.* III.7), "Knowing the knower generated by *Brahman*...attains the peace eternally" (*Ka.* I.I.17), "Knowing That in this way...the strings of death are severed" (*Śve.* IV.15), "The ancient gods and seer sages who had realized It, saturated with That, in truth achieved immortality" (*Śve.* V.6), "The resolute sages who realize It will have continuous peace, and not the others" (*Ka.* II.II.13).

[While for the *Smṛti* there are these passages:] "One who has conquered the *buddhi* abandons all meritorious and non-meritorious action" (*Bha. Gī.* II.50), "The sages who renounce the fruit of the action, with the *buddhi* conquered and free from the bond of births, rise to the blissful region" (*Bha. Gī.* II.51), "...you will be able to overcome all errors by ferrying yourself on the raft of knowledge" (*Bha. Gī.* IV.36), "...thus, O Arjuna, the fire of knowledge reduces all actions to ashes" (*Bha. Gī.* IV.37), "This highly secret science has been revealed by Me, O Anagha. He who realizes it will become sage and nothing will be left for him to accomplish" (*Bha. Gī.* XV.20), "...thus, having known me in reality, one immediately enters into Me" (*Bha. Gī.* XVIII.55), "The Knowledge of the *ātman* is considered the best of all [the forms of knowledge]: in fact it is the highest of all sciences because, truly, [only through it] Immortality is achieved. Only by realizing that [Knowledge], the 'Twice-born' becomes perfectly accomplished, and not by any other means. One who through the *ātman* thus realizes the *ātman* in all beings, having achieved equanimity towards everything, realizes the eternal *Brahman*. That one who is endowed with the authentic knowledge is no longer bound by action, while one who is devoid of knowledge is destined to continuous existential peregrination. The being born [in corporeal form] is made slave by action and liberated by knowledge: for this, the sages who have higher knowledge do not engage in *karman*" (*Ma. Bhā. Śā.* 241.7, *Bra. Pu.* 237.7), "The sages who possess the real knowledge state that the knowledge is the supreme good; in fact, pure knowledge liberates from all errors" (*Ma. Bhā. Ā.* 50.3), "Thus, having recognized that death re-occurs continuously, the knower draws from the eternal Light [*Brahman*] through knowledge. In truth, apart [from this], for him there is no other way. Meditating on That, the sage becomes perfectly pacified," "For the 'knower of the field' [the *jīva*], the purity [attained] through knowledge of the Lord represents the highest [form of] consciousness," "In truth, this is the supreme *dharma*: the realization of the *ātman* by means of *yoga*," "The knower of the *ātman* has overcome pain. He has no fear of anything, neither of the nearing of death, nor of death itself. He fears absolutely nothing," "He is not born, nor does he die; he is not killed, nor does he kill. He is not made a slave, nor does he make [others] slaves. He is not liberated, nor does he grant liberation. In truth, the [individual] *puruṣa* is the supreme *ātman*, and all that is different from That is non-real."

It having been ascertained that the *Śruti*, the *Smṛti* and the *Itihāsas* speak about the knowledge as the sole means to Liberation, it is opportune, therefore, that the *Upaniṣad* [whose purpose is to demonstrate the way of knowledge] should begin.

Besides, the same etymological derivation of the term *upaniṣad* indicates that only knowledge constitutes the discipline to achieve the supreme Goal of human existence. In fact, in this sense, it is considered that [the term] *upaniṣad*, formed of the root *sad* [to sit, to extinguish], preceded by the prefixes *upa* [= near] and *ni* [= completely], takes the meaning of "dispersing" [the ignorance], "achieving" [the knowledge-liberation] or "bringing to fulfillment" [the Goal of the human being]. With the term *upaniṣad,* therefore, knowledge (*vidyā*) is indicated: it constitutes the object dealt with in the Scripture that is about to be exposed; therefore, having the same purpose, the related text is called *Upaniṣad.*

This [knowledge] is designated *Upaniṣad* because it crushes and destroys the seed of the cyclical becoming (*saṁsāra*), which consists of ignorance, etc., in those questers for liberation who have lost all thirst for the objects seen [on earth] or about which they have heard from the Scriptures [as existing in other spheres]. They seek this knowledge expressed by the term *upaniṣad* with absolute firmness and resoluteness.

The knowledge of *Brahman* is also called *Upaniṣad* for the further reason that it leads these [questers] to realize the supreme *Brahman* and dissolves for them the possibility of unhappiness, such as dwelling in a womb, experiencing birth, aging, death, etc., allowing them to achieve the Supreme Good, superior to any other achievement.

Objection: The following objection can be raised: Accepting that knowledge is the only means to achieve liberation, then the teachings of the *Upaniṣad* that state that same knowledge can be justified; but it is not so because based on the following passages: "Offered up the *soma,* we became immortal" (*Ṛ.* 8.48.3, *Tai. Saṁ.* 3.2.5.4), "In truth, the good result for one who performs the four-monthly sacrifices certainly becomes indestructible" (*Śa. Brā.* 2.6.3.1)[1] and others, it is also recognized that the action (*karma* = sacrifice) grants liberation.

Answer: [This objection] cannot be accepted as valid, because it contradicts the *Śruti* and the *Smṛti* and is also in contrast with reason. First of all, the contradiction with the *Śruti* [is brought into evidence by passages such as the following and others]: "...as here is exhausted the condition obtained with the action [sacrificial rites], likewise in the other world is exhausted the condition obtained with the merit" (*Chā.* VIII.I.6), "One who so realizes That becomes immortal here [in this body]" (*Nṛ.* 1.6, *Tai. Ā.* VI.1.6), "There is no other way that leads us there" (*Śve.* III.8, VI.15, *Śu. Ya. U. Nā.* 31.17), "Some attained Immortality not with action, nor with progeny or wealth, but with detachment" (*Kai.* 3, *Ma. Nā.* 10.5), "Because these eighteen constituents of the sacrifice, on which it is said the lower rite is [founded], are perishable because they are precarious, those unwary people who think 'this is the supreme good' certainly proceed repeatedly toward old age and death" (*Mu.* I.II.7), "...from them there is detachment by recognizing that what is perishable cannot achieve that which is eternal" (*Mu.* I.II.12).

[Regarding the refutation on the part of the *Smṛti* there are these passages:] "The being is made a slave by action and freed by knowledge. Therefore the ascetics who saw the ultimate Reality do not engage in the *karman*" (*Ma. Bhā. Śā.* 241.7), "Having been impregnated with the impurities of ignorance, the ancient [*ātman*] is considered to be impure. In truth, only from the destruction of such [ignorance] can liberation be attained, and not otherwise, [not even] through the most excellent rituals" (*Li. Pu. Dhyā.* 56.89-90), "For the sages, liberation does not come from progeny, activity or even from riches. Liberation is attained only by means of detachment. Take notice: failing that, one continues wandering!" (*Li. Pu. Kā.* 86.20), "When the actions are performed, attachment to the fruits of such actions develops; therefore one continues to perform them and death is not overcome" (*Ma. Bhā. U.* 42.9), "The sage attains the eternal Light through Knowledge. For him, in truth, there is no other way"; "Thus, faithful to the doctrine of the three *Vedas*, they, desirous to enjoy, obtain the coming and going" (*Bha. Gī.* IX.21), "In reality, also the stages of life relating to the social orders are nothing but conditions [in which there is prescription] of activity. The *ātman* cannot be realized through the fulfillment of the duties pertaining to a specific stage, or through the *Vedas*, or with the sacrifices or even with the *Sāmkhya* or with the vows, or again with the many types of rigorous ascetic disciplines or with the manifold forms of donation. The knowers achieve It through the *ātman* itself" (*Li. Pu. Dhyā.* 56.46-47), "The *dharma* expressed in the three [*Vedas*] resolves itself in *adharma* and is quite similar to a fruit of *kimpāka* [beautiful to the sight but not edible]. There is, my dear, no [real] happiness here [in this world], saturated with innumerable pains. Therefore, how can I, who aspire to liberation, submit to the threefold [ritual science of the *Vedas*]?," "It is said that the human being, bound by the fetters of ignorance, is enslaved. Knowledge puts an end to such [ignorance], as light dispels darkness. Therefore Liberation is attained with knowledge, which totally resolves the ignorance," "The vows, the charitable offerings, the austerities, the sacrifices and the rectitude, [pilgrimages to] the sacred places, the ritual duties connected with the stages of life and the forms of *yoga* are finalized only to [the achievement of] the heavenly world and are impure and impermanent. [Only] knowledge is permanent and is bearer of total peace and allows the realization of the Great [Being, *Brahman*]," "Through sacrifices [man] attains divine nature, through austerities the sphere of *Brahmā*, through donations the enjoyment of various pleasurable things. But liberation is attained only through knowledge," "With the rope of rectitude, one proceeds toward heaven; with the rope of error, one descends to hell. But cutting both with the sword of knowledge, one becomes free from [contact with] the body and attains peace" (*Ma. Bhā. Śā.* 329.40), "Detach yourselves from the *dharma* and the *adharma*, leave the [apparent] real and the non-real behind. Once detached from the [apparent] real and from the non-real, detach from that through which you detached" (*Ma. Bhā, Śā.* 331.44).

Thus the *karman* does not constitute a means to [attain] Immortality, because such a point of view is in contrast with both the *Śruti* and the *Smṛti* and also with logic.

If liberation were achieved through action, then it would be subject to the four phases concerning the action [production, acquisition, purification and transformation] and therefore would be impermanent. But it is never noted that what is obtained through the action has eternal nature; all that is produced by action is impermanent, and the supporters of all the doctrines admit that liberation is eternal.

The *Śruti*, in one of its ritualistic chapters, with regard to the four-monthly sacrificial rites, states: "O living creature, your immortality rests precisely in returning repeatedly into existence as living creature!" (*Tai. Brā.* 1.5.5.6).

Besides, [in the *Smṛti*] regarding the [merit deriving from the] right action (*sukṛta*) [of those who celebrate the four-monthly sacrifices, there is the passage]: "...it is said that the merit becomes imperishable," where the term "merit" refers to the action.

Objection: In this case, being the means for the attainment of the divine condition, etc., the actions would be precisely the cause of the condition of slavery.

Answer: True. By their nature they are the cause of slavery. In this sense there are these passages of the *Śruti*: "...the world of the Fathers [is attained] with the rite" (*Br.* I.V.16), "All these [who practice the three branches of the merit] become [qualified to attain] virtuous worlds..." (*Chā.* II.XXIII.1), "Believing the sacrifice and the meritorious actions to be the best thing, the lacking ones do not comprehend anything else of preeminence. After having experienced in the heavens' vertex the meritorious fruit, they come to this world or to a lower one" (*Mu.* I.II.10).

[Instead the passages from the *Smṛti* are:] "...So, some, who know the Essence, are not attached to the actions: in the *Smṛti* there is mention that the human being is consubstantiated of knowledge and not made of action" (*Ma. Bhā. Ā.* 51.32), "So, faithful to the doctrine of the three *Vedas*, desiring enjoyment, they obtain the coming and going" (*Bha. Gī.* IX.21).

But if the work is performed by offering it to the Lord without any desire for the fruit, then [the same action] is the cause of purification of the heart. This produces the knowledge that determines liberation. So the action without attachment causes the attainment of liberation through gradual steps.

In this sense the Lord [Kṛṣṇa] says: "One who, transcending attachment, acts dedicating his works to *Brahma*, remains free from error like a lotus leaf in the middle of a pond. For the purification of the ego, the *yogis* [those who follow *Karmayoga*] perform their actions with the body, the mind, the higher intellect or also just with the senses, renouncing the attachment" (*Bha. Gī.* V.10-11), "Whatever you do, whatever you eat, whatever you offer in sacrifice, whatever you give, whatever effort of austerity you perform, O Kaunteya, do it as if you were in debt to Me. In this way you will be freed from the bonds of the *karma* that produces good or bad fruits; free, with the mind concentrated on the *yoga* of renunciation, you will reach Me" (*Bha. Gī.* IX.27-28).

Liberation is impossible without the purification of the heart. The heart is purified by action. This is the process described also in the sacred *Viṣṇudharma* to attain liberation by stages: "First of all the *yogin* studies [the *Vedas*], then he performs the sacrifices; after that he renounces the ritual activity and finally he becomes qualified for the knowledge that leads to liberation. In this way he is freed step by step... Until the errors accumulated over manifold births have been completely exhausted, the mind of the human being does not turn to Govinda [*Brahman*]. In those people who have attenuated their errors through austerity, knowledge and contemplation for thousands of successive births, there develops the devotion toward Kṛṣṇa. In truth, here [the mind, which is] the receptacle [of the impressions] of the erroneous actions constitutes an impediment for final liberation. Therefore, one who fears existential becoming must make an intense effort to bring under control the same [mind]. Such a pacification is attained through the donations of one's riches like gold, etc., through bathing in sacred waters and with the practice of great corporeal austerities, as prescribed in the Scriptures. The snare of the error is loosened also by prayer to the *devas*, by hearing of the sacred Scriptures, by pilgrimage to the sacred places and by service rendered to one's Master."

Also Yājñavalkya speaks of the need to purify [the mind] to attain [liberation] and of the method to obtain that [purification]: "In truth, the purification of the heart must be worked particularly by the mendicant monk (*bhikṣu*), being the means to cultivate the knowledge that leads to liberation" (*Yā. Ya.* 62), "In fact, as a mirror made opaque by impurities cannot reflect any images, so a [mental] organ, if not purified, is not able to unveil the knowledge of the *ātman*" (*Yā. Ya.* 1.4.1), "The *yogin* realizes the immortality after having purified the heart with the following means: adoration regarding the spiritual preceptor, investigation into the meaning of the Vedic Scriptures, fulfillment of the right actions, keeping in sacred company, the purifying invocations; dismissal of women from sight and contact, perception of the *ātman* in all beings, detachment [from the fruit of actions] and non-acceptance [of gifts, etc.], wearing old clothes made of rough ocher-color cloth; retiring of the senses from enjoyment of objects, repression of phlegm and indolence, awareness of the real nature of the physical body, acknowledgment of the evil innate in the tendency to act [egoistically]; the purification of the mind from *rajas* and *tamas*, the [sensorial and mental] pacification and the absence of contact [of the organs with the objects and of the mind with the thoughts relating to them]" (*Yā. Ya*. 156-159), "Where the study of the *Vedas* and of the *Purāṇas*, the meditation (*vidyā*) and the comprehension of the *Upaniṣads* [are direct means to realize knowledge of the *ātman*], in a similar way [the study regarding] the *ślokas*, the *sūtras*, the *bhāṣyas* and wherever else there is oral expression, but also the recitation of the *Vedas*, the performance of the sacrifices, the practice of the *brahmacarya* and of the austerities, the control of the senses, the faith [in the words of the Teacher and in the Scriptures], the fasting and the non-dependence on others also constitute [indirect] means for the attainment of the Knowledge of the *ātman*" (*Yā. Ya*. 189-190).

In this sense, also in the *Atharva* [*Veda*], it is shown that knowledge of the *ātman* descends from perfect mental purification: "But once the accumulated errors have been extinguished through thousands of births, then they see in the *yoga* [the means to obtain] the total uprooting of the existential becoming" (*Yo.* I.78-79), "When the mind has been made perfectly pure and devoid of attachment [toward the objects], the monks whose errors have been attenuated [by the discipline, etc.] see [everything] as *ātman*."

The *Bṛhadāraṇyaka* [*Upaniṣad*] also speaks of the sacrifice and of other [ritual practices] as means to satisfy the compelling need for knowledge: "The *brāhmaṇas* intend to know That through the study of the *Vedas* and by means of sacrifice, offerings, ascetic discipline and fasting" (*Bṛ.* IV.IV.22).

Objection: From the following passage of the Scripture, it is learned that action also is a means to attain immortality: "One who knows the two [ways], knowledge and non-knowledge, together..." (*Ī.* 11). Also the following passage [of the *Smṛti*], likewise, maintains this opinion: "For the sage, both austerity and knowledge are a means to attain the Supreme Good."

Answer: It is true [that action is a means to Liberation], but it is not a direct means. Certainly it is recognized that [liberation] is attained through the purification of the heart, and that is attained through such [action].

Thus, in fact, the two passages mentioned earlier, that is: "In fact, one who knows the two [ways], knowledge and non-knowledge...," etc., and "For the sage, both austerity and knowledge are a means to attain the Supreme Good," etc., undoubtedly state that both knowledge and action are able to determine attainment of the Supreme Good.

It can be asked: How is this possible?

The closing sentence of every quotation gives the answer. The quotation of the *Upaniṣad* ends clearly showing that the action [which is based on ignorance] is only cause for annulment of the error, while [only] knowledge is means to attain immortality: "...having overcome death through non-knowledge, one reaches immortality through knowledge" (*Ī.* 11), while [the closing part of the second quotation, the one drawn from the *Smṛti*, is]: "They destroy the error with the austerity and attain immortality with knowledge."[2]

Where [in whatever section of the *Vedas* the fulfillment of the action is described but] any instruction regarding the purification [of the mind], etc., as its indirect result, is not provided, precisely there the completion [based on the mention of such result] with other sections [of the *Vedas*, in which that is described in an exhaustive manner] must be applied.[3]

Objection: Anyway, there is the passage [of the Scriptures]: "Only by performing here the rites (*karman*) can one desire to live a hundred years" (*Ī.* 2) requires us to commit to the performance of the ritual activity for the entire life. Therefore, how is it possible to attain liberation only by means of knowledge [not accompanied by the action]?

Answer: This norm is applied only to one who is qualified for the ritual action and not to the knower of *Brahman*, who has transcended the necessity of the action [and even the qualification to perform the ritual activity]: this one cannot be submitted to any obligation. In this sense, the *Śruti* itself indicates that the performance of the action cannot be imposed on the knower: "No one can order a knower to perform ritual activity, not even a *ṛṣi*, nor to submit to the scriptural injunctions or to abide by the Scriptures [regarding the action]. Precisely because of this, in truth, the ancient sages did not celebrate the *Agnihotra* sacrifice" (*Kau. Brā.* 2.4), "In truth, knowing the *ātmā* in this way, the *brāhmaṇas*, abandoning desire for progeny, yearning for prosperity and the aspiration to dominate the worlds, then undertake the mendicant life" (*Bṛ.* III.V.1), "The *ṛṣis* of the Kavaṣi lineage, knowing this same [*ātman*], in truth, said: Why should we ever study [the *Vedas*]? Why should we ever celebrate sacrifices?" (*Ai. Ā.* 3.2.6.12), "Therefore, thanks to what has he become a knower of *Brahman*? Thanks to whatever thing [he became that], he is always that" (*Bṛ.* III.V.1).

Likewise the Lord [Kṛṣṇa in the *Bhagavadgītā*] expresses himself: "But for that one who finds his joy only in the *ātman*, who is satisfied in the *ātman* and who finds his peace in the *ātman*, there is no other duty to be performed. Neither action (*kṛtena*) nor non-action will ever interest such a being in this world; he depends on no one; nor, for any purpose, can he find refuge in other beings" (*Bha. Gī.* III.17-18).

Also the supreme Lord [Śiva] expressed himself in a similar manner in the *Liṅga* [*Purāṇa*], through the narration of the story of Kālakūṭa: "The sage, who by means of this Knowledge has uprooted the attachment, even if living in a body, has no more duty to fulfill, O highest among the sages; if, on the other hand, something is left in him, then this one is not a knower of the Reality. Certainly for him, there is nothing to be performed either in this world or in the next, because in reality the knower of *Brahman* is truly a liberated in life. In fact, having realized the ultimate Essence, he remains always immersed in the actuality of the knowledge and detached [from all the rest]. Having abandoned the notion of duty, he is absorbed solely in knowledge. O supreme among the 'Twice-born,' the fool, instead, rejecting the knowledge, identifies with the social orders and the stages of life and experiences pleasure in other things: he is the victim of ignorance, there is no doubt about this. In truth, those who [still blinded by ignorance] continue to act under the influence of anger, of fear, and also of greed and illusion, of the idea of separation, of arrogance and of laziness and furthermore of rectitude and wickedness, because of this [after death] they repeatedly take bodies corresponding [to those inclinations]" (*Li. Pu. Kā.* 86.105-109), "In truth, suffering continues as long as the body lasts; this is why ignorance should be uprooted. For the *yogin* who right here [during the existence of the body] has eliminated ignorance by means of knowledge, anger and the other [impurities] are destroyed, while also merit and demerit reach their end. So, upon their destruction, he does not associate himself again with a body, and freed from the threefold unhappiness [due to the body and to the natural and supranatural sphere], he becomes totally liberated from existential becoming" (*Li. Pu. Kā.* 86.112-14).

Similarly, in the *Śivadharmottara* [one reads]: "The *yogin* who, perfectly fulfilled by the nectar of knowledge, has nothing else to accomplish, is beyond every duty. If he still has [the notion of something to carry out], then he would not be a knower of Reality. For him, in both worlds nothing exists any longer that must be carried out. Right here he is completely liberated, becoming perfect Fullness and attaining equanimity of vision towards all." Therefore, this injunction relating to the fulfillment of the ritual action [for a hundred years, contained in the passage]: "Only performing here the rites (*karman*)...," etc. (*Ī.* 2), applies to one who is immersed in ignorance [and not to the knower, because the latter is free from the notion of duty].

Besides, it should also be noted that the statement [of the *Īśā Upaniṣad*]: "Only performing here the rites (*karman*)..." is not used in that context as an injunction relating to the ritual action; it only means that [a person endowed with knowledge] can act, if he so desires, demonstrating the glory of knowledge itself. What is said means: a *jñānin,* even though he engages in the action through his entire life, according to his will and in a way [for the others apparently] meritorious or non-meritorious, does not get any maculation because [of attachment to the fruits] of action precisely by virtue of the power of knowledge.

In fact the *Veda* [*Upaniṣad*] begins with the statement: "*Oṁ*! The Lord [*parameśvara*] pervades [being its foundation] all that exists and all that changes in the universal movement..." (*Ī.* 1) [which means that the *jñānin* should consider the entire universe as *Brahman*]. The *Upaniṣad*, continuing, states: "Having thus deposed [all attachment], care for [what you are]" (*ibid.*), where it is evident that it advises the knower to protect the *ātman* through detachment from all actions. Therefore it would not be pertinent that [the *Upaniṣad*] repeat the necessity of performing detachment on the part of the knower of *Brahman* who is, anyway, beyond all injunctions.

In reality [the *Upaniṣad*] by saying: "Only performing here the rites (*karman*)..." (*Ī.* 2) hesitates to advise the *jñānin* to renounce his duty. In the continuation of the passage: "...one can desire to live a hundred years" (*ibid.*), the idea is that he can commit himself for his entire life to various actions as they present themselves in the empirical world, i.e., both pleasurable and unpleasurable, etc.; that is, he should not stay inactive after having abandoned his own duties, etc., for fear of remaining conditioned by merit, etc. "For you" (*ibid.*), who are knower, and "...[intend to live] so" (*ibid.*), though continuing to perform action, there is no (*na asti*) change of condition (*anyathā*)—like falling from your intrinsic nature, or remaining imprisoned in *saṁsāra* because of merit, etc.—that is due (*itaḥ*) to having performed the duties throughout your entire life.

An alternative interpretation can be: "...from this [action]..." there is no (*na asti*), i.e., [due to having performed that action, even for the entire life] there will not be in a future time, the acquisition of a different condition (*anyathā*) as remaining entangled in *saṁsāra*, because the action (*karman*) offered [to the Lord, therefore performed without attachment to its fruits] cannot adhere to you (*tvayi na lipyate*).[4]

There are also other passages of the *Śruti* with the same meaning: "...one is no longer touched by the unworthy action" (*Bṛ.* IV.IV.23), "...the erroneous action no longer attaches to one who so knows" (*Chā*. IV.XIV.3), "The actions performed and those missed no longer torment him" (*Bṛ*. IV.IV.22), "...all the errors of that one performing the Agnihotra, knowing that, are burnt instantly" (*Chā*. V.XXIV.3).

[Also the *Bhagavadgītā* states:] "Thus...the fire of knowledge (*jñāna*) reduces all actions to ashes" (*Bha. Gī*. IV.37).

In the *Liṅgapurāṇa* one reads: "All actions of the knower come to dissolution: of this there is no doubt" (*Li. Pu. Kā*. 86.118), and also in the *Śivadharmottara* we find: "Therefore, having cut off promptly and completely with the sword of knowledge the tie of the action, performed with or without desire, and having become pure, he dwells established in the *ātman*. As a great blazing fire burns everything, what is dry and also what is humid, so the fire of knowledge burns instantly both the pure and the impure action. As a lotus leaf, which is not wetted by the little drops of water that settle on it, the knower is not touched by the water of the objects, like sound and others. As one who is protected by the power of the *mantras* is not bitten by snakes, not even if he is playing with them, so he is not touched by the sensorial snakes even while he is enjoying them. As a poison ingested is annihilated by the power of the *mantras* and of the medicines, in the same way all the errors of the knower are destroyed instantly."

In the same way, also the compiler of the *sūtras* [Bādarāyana-Vyāsa] in the following passage asserts that only Knowledge constitutes the means for [attainment of] the supreme goal of the human being: "The [attainment of the] supreme goal of the human being descends from such [knowledge as it is given by the *Vedas*]; [this is comprehended] from the scriptural testimony. Thus states Bādarāyaṇa" (*Bra. Sū.* 3.4.1).

Then, [by raising a potential objection from an apparent adversary of the Jaimini school], in the subsequent aphorism he states that the action (*karman*) depends in any case upon the agent (*kartṛ*) [and on other factors as the Divinity, the means, the fruit, etc., whereby the Scriptures that prescribe the knowledge would appear of secondary and not fundamental importance]: "Because [the knowledge of the *ātman* as imparted by the *Upaniṣads*] constitutes an integral part [of rites, etc., its fruit] consists in the glorification of the human being [performing them], as happens in other [cases]," etc. (*Bra. Sū.* 3.4.2).

So, the question arisen that the knowledge constitutes something complementary to the ritual activity, the subsequent *sūtra*: "Instead, by virtue of the instruction that puts [the *ātman* as] the Supreme [Entity], for Bādarāyaṇa it is so...," etc. (*Bra. Sū.* 3.4.8), establishes that, because it is taught that *Brahman* is completely distinct from those properties that characterize the cyclical becoming, such as the function of agent and the other [conditions necessary for the action] and has a nature uncontaminated by error, etc., the one who has already realized That [*Brahman*], no longer has to pursue the discipline of the action.

In fact, precisely because of the nature of the field where the action is performed—that is to say the universal totality itself [apparently differentiated and] consisting in the action, the agent and the fruit, whose manifestation is produced by ignorance—one realizes its end in the intrinsic substance by the power of knowledge; in other words, there is the defect consisting in the failing of the very requisites necessary for the fulfillment of the action. So [the knower of *Brahman*] can no longer conceive [between knowledge and ritual action] a relationship of reciprocal complementarity [in the attainment of the Supreme Good], nor postulate either a possible harmonization [as if they were fufilling the same goal] or even a relationship similar to that between a principal and a secondary element [that is to say, one being the auxiliary of the other].

To confirm this, [the *Brahmasūtra*] discusses [the knowledge and the action] in two separate sections, and their results are not the same. [In the *sūtra*:] "And precisely for this there is no obligation regarding [the fulfillment of rites like the one concerning] the starting of the fire and other [rites for the renouncers]" (*Bra. Sū.* 3.4.25), [Vyāsa concludes] that knowledge alone is the means to [realize] the supreme goal of human existence. In order for knowledge to produce its fruit [that is, liberation, there should not be resorting to any action and] the rituals prescribed for a specific stage of life, like the starting of the fire, etc., must no longer be taken into consideration.

This in synthesis is the result [of the discussion] in the section just mentioned [*Bra. Sū.* 3.4], where the absolute independence [of the knowledge in leading to liberation] was also demonstrated.

Now, in the subsequent *sūtra*: "Besides, due to the [testimony of the] *Śruti* regarding the sacrifice, etc., [is in force] the obligation regarding all [the religious duties], as in the case of the horse" (*Bra. Sū.* 3.4.26), it seems instead to be affirmed that it is not totally independent [from the action].

In fact, although once knowledge has been acquired, it does not depend on anything to produce its fruit [liberation], yet until its dawning there is dependence [on the action as prerequisite to knowledge], as learned from the *Śruti*: "The *brāhmaṇas* intend to know That through the study of the *Vedas* and through sacrifice, offerings, ascetic discipline and fasting" (*Bṛ.* IV.IV.22). As such is affirmed the usefulness of the action as means to induce the aspiration to knowledge. Therefore, in the two *sūtras*: "It is not so because there is no specification whatever" and "Or the participation [in the ritual action] is intended in order to celebrate [knowledge]" (*Bra. Sū.* 3.4.13-14), [Vyāsa] demonstrates that the *mantra*: "Only performing here the rites (*karman*)..." (*Ī.* 2) possesses a twofold meaning: it refers to the non-knower and besides [the action is mentioned because] it expresses praise with regard to knowledge.

Therefore, because, based on what has been exposed, [it is evident] that knowledge alone constitutes the means for liberation, it is good to start propounding the *Upaniṣad*.

Objection: If the bondage [of the *jīva*] were unreal, then it could be destroyed by knowledge alone and we could also expect to attain immortality by means of knowledge. But it is not so, because [the bondage of the *jīva*, although not yet ascertained] is effectively perceived [as, also, multiplicity itself is a question of universal perception]. Secondly, there cannot be any elimination [of such bondage, its unreality not having been proved]. Thirdly, one becomes aware of the *ātman* through concepts such as "you" ("I," etc.) but, as the *ātman* by its own nature is quite distinct [from anything else] and, there being no affinity [with any other, as there is no other entity that, similar to the *ātman*, transcends all the concepts, and because the similarity is the only base of the superimposition, in absence of such similarity] no superimposition is conceivable [therefore the bondage, or *saṁsāra*, cannot be described as unreal].[5]

Answer: Both real and unreal objects are perceived. As perception is the factor common to both, an entity cannot be called real simply because it is perceived. [Bondage] cannot [be maintained to be] real only because of the [presumed] impossibility of eliminating it: in fact its suppression is very plausible from both the perspective of the scriptural injunctions and the perspective of causality. So the non-reality of the phenomenal world is directly asserted by the *Śruti*, which precisely speaks of it as apparent, as it is the result of *māyā*: "...but there is no second distinct from it..." (*Bṛ.* IV.III.23), "...which troubling, which affection [can there be] for that one who recognizes himself as [supreme] unity?" (*Ī.* 7), "When [the supreme Reality] is known, the duality does not exist [any longer]" (*Mā. Kā.* I.18), "Whence ever [would duality draw its being?...]" since "...beyond That there is nothing that has to be known, having recognized everything as *Brahman*" (*Śve.* I.12), "One only without a second" (*Chā.* VI.II.1), "...each modification of it is nothing but mere denomination of name" (*Chā.* VI.I.4), "The real Being is one only" (*A.* 63), "In That there is no multiplicity"

(*Bṛ.* IV.IV.19), "In one way only it must be realized..." (*Bṛ.* IV.IV.20), "*Prakṛti* must be recognized, in truth, as *māyā*..." (*Śve.* IV.10), "The Possessor of *māyā* manifests this universe..." (*Śve.* IV.9), "*Indra*, through *māyā*, is perceived as of manifold form...," etc. (*Bṛ* II.V.19).

[In the *Bhagavadgītā* we read:] "Although I am the non-born and indestructible *ātman*, although I am the Lord of all creatures, founded on my own nature, I come into existence by the power of *māyā*" (*Bha. Gī.* IV.6), "Although undivided, nevertheless it appears divided" (*Bha. Gī.* XIII.16).

Similarly, also in the *Brahma Purāṇa*, we read: "Imaginary concepts such as birth and death, pleasure and pain, merit and demerit do not certainly exist in the *Puruṣa*, which is the ultimate Reality. The *Puruṣa* is also free from the conditions of the social orders, from the stages of life and from the very celestial life (heaven) or infernal life. The unreal world appears, through the error [induced by *māyā*], real...as for a thirsty animal the water of a mirage in the desert, as the silver that seems hard metal, or as the mother of pearl in the oyster shell that looks like silver, or as a piece of rope on the floor that in the darkness of a room appears as a snake. Other examples of similar illusions are the moon in the sky that, although one, appears as if it were double to one affected by diplopia, or as the appearance of solidity, the transparency or the blue of the sky. As the sun, sole, appears manifold [when reflected] in several stretches of water, thus the supreme *ātman* [which is non-dual] appears existing [in a manifold way] through the limiting superimpositions (*upādhi*). The false perception of duality, denominated ignorance, is pure imagination; it is non-real. Those, who through ignorance erroneously identify the body with the *ātman*, create for themselves a corporeal prison in the future existence. [All the phenomenal experiences] at the beginning, in the middle and at the end are included [at an individual level] in *viśva*, *taijasa*, and *prājña* [and at the universal level in *Virāj*, *Hiraṇyagarbha* and *Īśvara*] that remain always apparently concealed by the three states of waking, dreaming and deep sleep [respectively]. Through the same *māyā*, in the form of duality, one creates confusion in oneself, but also realizes *Hari*, which is one's own *ātman* concealed in the depth of the heart. *Viṣṇu's* own nature manifests itself in creation as boundless duality in manifold forms like lightning, fires, flashes and rays of light in the sky. [The nature of the world of duality is such that] when the mind becomes quiet, the Lord (*Īśvara*) is perceived, always and everywhere, as perfect quiet, while when the mind becomes troubled and dull also It appears as such [troubled and dull]. Yet It never has that nature.

"The modifications of iron, a piece of clay or gold have no reality; likewise the diversity of living and non-living creatures is [only apparent and] non-real, but igorance (*avidyā*), being founded on the *ātman*, which is consciousness, omnipresent and devoid of support, having taken the *ātman* as support, creates the dual manifestation. As a snake is never a rope, nor a rope ever a snake, so there is no cause even for the coming into existence or the destruction of the world. This ignorance has been conceived for the empirical experience of the worlds. This same [ignorance], in the form of duality and non-duality, is said to be the cause of the illusion. One should always contemplate *Brahman* as non-dual, entire and undivided. The knower of the *ātman*, who has transcended pain, has nothing more to be worried about, neither fear of death when facing *Mṛtyu* [*Yama*] nor the fear of anything else. He is not born nor does he die, he is not killed nor does he kill. He is not made aslave, nor does he make slaves [of others]. He is not liberated, nor does he grant liberation. In truth, the [individual] *puruṣa* is the supreme *ātman*, and all that is different from That is non-real. Having thus comprehended what is the nature of the world, which consists of the *māyā* of *Viṣṇu* and is apparent, one has to free oneself from attachment to experience, having detached from all mental projections. Having abandoned all mental projections, having rendered the mind immobile and having fixed it on his own *ātman*, the *yogin* must remain pacified as a fire that has exhausted its fuel. This *māyā* or primordial nature (*Prakṛti*), diversified into twenty-four cosmic principles [the categories of the *Sāṁkhya*], springs from That. From it come passion and anger, greed and illusion and also fear, despondency and suffering and the entire nest of imaginary ghosts, virtue and vice, pleasure and pain, transformations like creation and destruction, the way into hell, the dwelling in paradise, the conditions of birth and the stages of life, the attachment and the repulsion and the innumerable physical afflictions, childhood, youth and old age, separation and union, enjoyment, fasting and the vows. Endowed with this knowledge, the sage man should depose this [entire collection of projections] and live as a *muni* taking the vow of silence. Consider such a being as one of the right comprehension."

Here is a quotation from the *Viṣṇudharma*, a treatise in six chapters: "This 'knower of the field' [the *jīva*] under the enchantment of *māyā* without beginning thinks of itself as separated from *Brahman*, while it is really one with It. In truth, as long as the *jīva* perceives itself as other than the supreme *ātman*, until then, the creature, confused by his own acting, wanders incessantly. But when his action has been completely exhausted, he realizes the pure supreme *Brahman* as non-distinct from himself and, having become pure, he unveils as immortal. All actions are *avidyā*, while *vidyā* is considered [true] knowledge. The creature is born because of [its] action and is freed [from the corporeal prison] through *vidyā*. In truth, non-duality (*advaita*) is the supreme Reality, while duality is said to be its opposite. O king, also this fourfold differentiation of animals, vegetals, human nature and the infernal creatures has its root in the illusory ignorance. So is the ignorance, defined as 'duality' [because of which we think]: 'I am other,' 'he is other again [from me]' and 'these are distinct [from me].' But now listen regarding non-duality. Non-duality is realized as completely exempt from ideas like 'mine' and 'I,' as unconditioned, immutable and indefinable. Duality consists of mental conditions, while Non-duality is the supreme Reality. The states of mind are caused by *dharma* and by its opposite. They should be suppressed; at their suppression the [perception of] duality cannot emerge again. The entire universe of the living and of the inert entitites is only mental projection: in truth, when the mind resolves into silence, then non-duality is realized. The same thought that is present in the actions constitutes an obstacle in [the attainment of the Knowledge of the] *Brahman*. In the way in which we think about the actions, so arises an awareness of the same kind. Certainly, as is the conception [that one nourishes], so becomes [one's] awareness. When this [thinking] is stopped, the supreme *Brahman* unveils solely by itself, without effort. Among the people, O *Indra*, the separation of oneself [in that *jīva*] from the supreme [*ātman*] is projected through ignorance. Thus, in truth, when that is destroyed, there is [evidence of the] non-separation between the *ātmā* [as the *jīva*] and the supreme [*ātman*]. The *ātmā* [in manifestation], when associated with the attributes (*guṇas*) of *Prakṛti*, is called the 'knower of the field' (*kṣetrajña*). Once pure, because not associated with those very attributes, it is proclaimed as the supreme *ātman*."

Likewise, also in the sacred *Viṣṇu Purāṇa* [we read]: "O Lord of the universe, only You are the supreme and sole *ātman*! There is no one else. That by which this [entire universe] of living and inert entities is pervaded is Your own glory. All that is perceived by those who are not *yogin*, like the tangible universe, is nothing but Yourself, Incarnation of the knowledge. They perceive the nature of the world through a fallacious knowledge. Those who have not recognized that this entire universe has the nature of pure knowledge, perceive it as an entity of material nature and wander in the ocean of illusion. But the sages, by the pure heart, realize that the entire universe is the Incarnation of knowledge; they consider it as the manifestation of your supreme Majesty" (*Vi. Pu.* 1.4.38-

41), "He who nourishes the conviction: 'I am *Hari*, and *Janārdana* and all this [universe]' and knows that all that consists in cause and effect is not other from himself will not be afflicted by the pair of opposites that come from being born [in corporeal form]" (*Vi. Pu.* 1.22.87), "The same one, from the perspective of the supreme Reality, unveils himself as absolutely clear as pure Consciousness, presents himself through an erroneous perception as if he had the nature of the material objects" (*Vi. Pu.* 1.2.6), "In truth, this Lord (*bhagavān*), who is pure consciousness and appears endowed with innumerable forms, has never become a material entity; therefore, recognize that the different [objects as] mountains, oceans and lands, etc., are manifestations of the awareness" (*Vi. Pu.* 2.12.39), "Can there ever exist, in some place, an object that is devoid of beginning, middle and end and that is eternally self-identical? O 'Twice-born,' how could all that on earth does not possess that nature and appears subject to change be defined as real? The clay can take the form of a vase, the vase [again manipulating the clay] can be transformed into a cup; the cup [once dried] can break into small fragments and these end up by crumbling into dust. Tell me, then: which real entity can be beheld here by those people whose certitudes regarding the *ātman* are obstructed by [their own] actions?[6] Therefore, O 'Twice-born,' there exists no real entity, in no place and in no time, irrespective of the awareness. What really exists is knowledge only, considered differently by different people, endowed with different minds, as the result of their respective past actions. The knowledge, which is perfectly pure, without stain, free from pain and exempt from any association with [feelings such as] greed, etc., is one only and is always identical to itself; It is the supreme Lord, It is *Vāsudeva*, beyond whom there is nothing. So, O Venerable, I expounded to you the nature of Being: it is pure knowledge and is also the Reality; the rest is non-real. But at the same time I have also revealed to you the nature of empirical contingency of what is in the world" (*Vi. Pu.* 2.12.41-45), "The *karman* is accumulated through ignorance, and this is valid for all living beings. But the *ātman* is pure, immutable, pacified, free from the *guṇas* and beyond *Prakṛti*. It is the very *ātman* that dwells in all creatures without undergoing any increase or decrease" (*Vi. Pu.* 2.13.70-71), "That only is the Essence, which will never be known by a different name as result of change or other [as modification, etc.]. O king, what is [this Essence]?" (*Vi. Pu.* 2.13.100), "O best among men, if somebody else existed apart from Myself, then I could say: 'I am this one' and 'that is him,' ...but when, in truth, a single Person dwells in all bodies, then expressions such as: 'Who are you?' and 'I am this' become devoid of foundation. That you are king, that this is your palanquin, that these are the bearers, that this is your kingdom—all of it, it can be said, is purely illusory" (*Vi. Pu.* 2.13.90-92), "King, warrior, regality and other similar concepts used in the practical life are all simple [non-real] mental projections" (*Vi. Pu.* 2.13.99), "The sages describe the supreme Reality as that which is not subject to destruction" (*Vi. Pu.* 2.14.24), "O Bhūpāla, listen: I will tell you in brief what is, in truth, the supreme Reality. It is the *ātman*, which is all pervasive, the same [in all creatures], pure, without attributes, beyond *Prakṛti* and free from change as birth, growth, etc., omnipresent, incorruptible... and of the essence of supreme knowledge. O Pārthiva, the supreme Lord has never been joined to names, or social orders, etc., nor is it now nor will it ever be in the future. It always has the same relationship with all bodies, with its own as well as with those of other [beings], a [relationship] that is never, from time to time, submitted to change. This is the highest knowledge; the dualists do not have this vision" (*Vi. Pu.* 2.14.28-31), "So, O sage, this entire universe is one [with the non-dual *Brahman*]. Its nature is the same as that of the supreme *ātman*, called *Vāsudeva*, and it has no separate existence [from Him]" (*Vi. Pu.* 2.15.35), "Also [a spiritual aspirant called] Nidāgha, having received the teaching of non-dualism, became devoted to it and as a result realized that all beings were nothing but the very *ātman*. Therefore, realizing identity with *Brahman*, O 'Twice-born,' he attained the final liberation" (*Vi. Pu.* 2.16.19), "As [the ignorant] considers the sky, which is sole, in various ways, as clear, blue, etc., so because of an erroneous perception also the *ātman*, although sole, appears singularly diversified [to different non-illuminated people]" (*Vi. Pu.* 2.16.20), "'Anything that is perceived here [in the universe] is only the immutable Lord. There is nothing that is other from That. I am That, you are That; all that exists is That, who has the nature of the *ātman*. Abandon the illusion of the distinction!' The great king, as the result of this teaching of that person, abandoned the [notion of] separateness and attained profound comprehension of the supreme Truth. He, again, regained the memory of his [past] births, obtained the final illumination and became liberated in this body" (*Vi. Pu.* 2.16.22-24).

Similarly, in the *Liṅgapurāna* one reads: "...therefore, in truth, that all the incarnated beings wander in *saṁsāra* is the result of ignorance. By reasoning, no difference is found between That which is free (the *ātman*) and that which seems to be dependent upon others (the *jīva*)" (*Li. Pu.* 86.16.95), "Certainly, not even unity exists at all: whence then, alas, could the duality ever be there? If there is neither the one nor any mortal, how could death manifest?" (*Li. Pu.* 86.16.96), "*That* is not conscious of the internal (subjective) world, nor is it conscious of the external (objective) world, nor is it conscious of both. It is not even a homogeneous mass of awareness; it is not simple consciousness, nor unconsciousness" (*Li. Pu.* 86.16.97), "When Knowledge is realized, nothing else is there to be known; then, from the perspective of the supreme Reality, *nirvāṇa* [as Supreme Good to attain] is realized. The totality [that presents itself as dual] comes from the doubling of the ignorance [as the double image of the moon for someone affected by diplopia]. Regarding that, there is no reasoning to be had!" (*Li. Pu.* 86.16.98-100), "O 'Twice-born' ones, neither knowledge nor bondage nor liberation can be referred to the *ātman*. In truth the *jīva* is neither a cause nor an effect due to a modification, nor is it itself a modification. This is *māyā*, which cannot be defined either as real or as non-real."

With analogous meaning, also the blessed Parāśara [states]: "From This [*ātman*], in truth, the universe is born, and into Him is re-absorbed. The Lord of *māyā*, tying himself [apparently] to the *māyā*, produces manifold forms. But [He himself] does not transmigrate in this way, nor cause the others to transmigrate. He is neither agent, nor enjoyer, neither the *prakṛti* nor the *puruṣa*. He is not the *māyā* nor the *praṇa*. In reality He is pure Consciousness. Therefore, in truth, the cyclical becoming of all incarnated beings has its root in ignorance. In truth, the *ātman* is eternal, omnipresent, immutable and devoid of any defect. That, which is one, appears to be manifold through his own power of *māyā*, but He is not so in his own nature. Therefore the sages who [having realized the *ātman*] took the vow of silence affirm Non-duality as supreme Reality and describe the universe as pure consciousness. People who have deformed vision see it, because of ignorance, as a real entity. The *ātman*, which is pure immutable Consciousness, is devoid of attributes and is all-pervasive, is perceived, in truth, in the form of material objects by people of imperfect comprehension. When they truly realize that from the perspective of the supreme Reality the *ātman* [the *jīva*] is the absolute *ātman* and that the duality is nothing but *māyā*, then they will attain peace. Therefore neither the phenomenal universe nor the existential wandering exists, but only Awareness exists."

Therefore, based both on the *Śruti* and other [texts] that expound the cause of names [and forms, etc., that appear to differentiate the entities] and on the [analysis of] its true nature, the phenomenal universe is rejected [as real entity]. From this it is comprehended that it has apparent nature. *Brahman*, on the other hand, is decribed as non-gross, etc.; therefore that which [like the universe] presents an opposite appearance, that is to say gross [etc.], is certainly non-real. An example can be this: because there is just one moon, seeing two moons [because of defective sight] represents a pure illusion.

Similarly, also the compiler of the aphorisms, in the *sūtra*: "A double nature for the supreme [*ātman*] cannot be even in virtue of the position, because everywhere [in the *Śruti* it is taught that *Brahman* is devoid of attributes]" (*Bra. Sū.* 3.2.11), establishes that from both the perspective of its own nature and that of the attributes, the coexistence of a double nature is impossible because it is contradictory,[7] whereby *Brahman* is only that which is totally devoid of qualification. Then when in the aphorism: "If it is objected that [*Brahman*] is not [of a sole nature] because of the distinction [with which it is described in the *Śruti*...]" (*Bra. Sū.* 3.2.12), raises a doubt [by a hypothetical opponent] based on the passages of the *Śruti* that speak of differences, whereas it is not admitted even the qualified *Brahman* [as real in the absolute], in the continuation of the same *sūtra*, that is: "[...it is answered that] it is not so, by virtue of the explicit negation of it [as it is uttered] singularly [relating to the various manifest aspects]" (*ibid.*), concludes that only [That] devoid of attributes can be accepted [as real in the absolute], since the *Śruti* itself refutes the differentiation, which is the result of the association with the *upādhis*, and because based on the authority of the *Śruti* that asserts the absence of distinction it is not legitimate to assume [*Brahman*] to be [really] endowed of qualification.

So in the following aphorism: "Besides, also others [affirm] so" (*Bra. Sū.* 3.2.13), [it clarifies that] the followers of some versions [of the *Vedas*] after having excluded the distinction maintain only the absence of the distinction [as it is learned from the following passages]: "Only with the mind [*buddhi*] It must be known. In That there is no multiplicity. Goes from death to death that one who here sees only multiplicity" (*Bṛ.* IV.IV.19, *Ka.* II.I.11), "In only one way it must be realized..." (*Bṛ.* IV.IV.20), "This must be realized precisely as eternally established in the *ātman*... having recognized everything as *Brahman*. When one recognizes *Brahman* as threefold, that is, consisting of the enjoyer, the object of enjoyment and the Regulator, everything is explained" (*Śve.* I.12).

And so it is established [by the *Śruti* itself] that the universal unfolding, consisting in all that is object of fruition, in the enjoyer and in He who controls, is in its own proper nature the sole *Brahman*.

Nevertheless, also after having clearly demonstrated the thesis of the absence of attributes, the following objection could be raised:

Objection: If [*Brahman*] cannot have both the nature [qualified and non-qualified, or differentiated and non-differentiated], as [logically] it possesses only one nature, why is it maintained that *Brahman* is only that one devoid of form and not the opposite?

Answer: [To this corresponds the aphorism:] "In truth [*Brahman* is] only that without attributes, because that is the prevailing [scriptural assertion]" (*Bra. Sū.* 3.2.14), in which it is expressed that *Brahman* must be realized as totally exempt from aspects such as form and other [attributes].

For what reason?

"...because that is the prevailing [scriptural assertion]" (*ibid.*), as it is learned from the following and other passages of the *Śruti*: "It is neither gross nor subtle, it is neither short nor long..." (*Bṛ.* III.VIII.8), "...That which is without sound, without contact, without form and not subject to decay" (*Ka.* I.III.15), "In truth, that which renders manifest name and form is called space (*ākāśa*). That, in which they are founded, is *Brahman*" (*Chā.* VIII.XIV.1), "That is this *Brahman*, without antecedent or consequent, without internal and without external: this *ātman*, by means of which the all is known, is *Brahman*. This is the teaching" (*Bṛ.* II.V.19); passages that expound *Brahman* in a prevailing way as That which transcends the universal manifestation and at the same time gives substance to it [reflecting itself as *ātman* in every single *jīva*].

Other passages having as their object *Brahman* as cause [therefore the qualified Being or *Brahman* "with attributes" (*saguṇa*)] do not have [That supreme, "devoid of attributes" (*nirguṇa*)] as principal argument; and the texts dealing with it as the principal object are certainly more relevant than those that do not expound It as primary argument.[8] Therefore *Brahman* must be realized as totally devoid of qualifications (*nirviśeṣa*) and not as endowed with qualification (*saviśeṣa*), because in such manner it is expounded by the texts of the *Śruti* that deal with It in a specific manner.

Objection: Now, once the thesis of the absence of qualification is established, what will be, then, the outcome of the scriptural assertions having as their object possessing a form [etc., on the part of *Brahman*]?

Answer: As that question arises, in the *sūtra*: "Besides [*Brahman*, although devoid of attributes] is like the light [that takes the shape, etc., of the objects illuminated], hence there is not [the risk of] a loss of meaning [for the Scriptures]" (*Bra. Sū.* 3.2.15), [Bādarāyaṇa-Vyāsa] shows that there is no contradiction in providing instruction regarding particular forms of *Brahman* as if it possessed various aspects, if that is done with meditation as its end. In fact, precisely in the same way in which the moon, the sun, etc., appear endowed with a certain multiplicity of forms as the result of the association with superimpositions such as the [surface of the] water, etc., so also *Brahman* appears under different forms when reflected into the *upādhis*. In this way the sentences that describe *Brahman* by manifold aspects do not undergo any loss of meaning.

So, after having stated the usefulness of the passages of the *Śruti* that speak of the [apparent] manifold forms [of *Brahman*], in that they have as object *Brahman* reflected into the *upādhis*, [the compiler] finally concludes that *Brahman*, in the end, is only the one devoid of qualification: "Also the Scriptures declare [that *Brahman* possesses] precisely that nature" (*Bra. Sū.* 3.2.16).

Now, with reference to the passage of the *Śruti*: "As a block of sea salt [thrown in the water into which it dissolves], which is without internal and without external, is in itself perfect, homogeneous in substance, likewise, my dear, this *ātman*, without internal and without external, is in itself perfect as absolute unity of pure knowledge" (*Bṛ.*

IV.V.13), in which it is established that [*Brahman*] has no other nature than that of pure consciousness-knowledge, appears in fact the aphorism: "Besides [the *Śruti* itself] illustrates [this meaning] and similarly also the *Smṛti* [reports it]" (*Bra. Sū.* 3.2.17).

So, based on the following and on other passages of the *Śruti* and of the *Smṛti*, it is established in unequivocal manner that *Brahman* is absolutely devoid of any differentiation: "...therefore, after that, there is the description [of *Brahman*] as: 'not this, not this'" (*Bṛ.* II.III.6), "That is other from the known and is also beyond the unknown" (*Ke.* I.3), "He who has realized... *Brahman*, from which words recede, together with thought, unable to grasp it..." (*Tai.* II.IV.1), "That Knowledge totally free from any differentiation, which is identified with pure Existence, which is beyond the reach of words and of which everyone is for himself conscious, is *Brahman*" (*Vi. Pu.* 6.7.53), "The characteristic of the supreme *ātman* is to be absolutely distinct from any form" (*Vi. Pu.* 6.7.54).

Having taken note of this, the following *sūtra* is now considered: "Therefore there are also comparisons as that [of the image] of the sun [in the water], etc." (*Bra. Sū.* 3.2.18).

Precisely for the reason that [the supreme *ātman*] has the nature of pure Consciousness, It is essentially defined by the formula "*neti, neti*: not this, not this" (*Bṛ.* II.III.6), therefore is other from the known and the unknown, is beyond the reach of words, is absolutely free from any kind of differentiation and is by its own nature completely distinct from any form, while all [apparent] distinction within the supreme *ātman* is due to the limiting superimpositions induced by ignorance [of its true nature]; therefore, in the Scriptures that deal with liberation is advanced the comparison of the sun [whose image is reflected] on the water, etc., bringing out that its [apparent] qualified condition, which does not correspond to the supreme Realty, has cause in such limiting superimpositions (*upādhis*): "In truth, as space, which is unique, appears in a diversified way in vases or other [containers], so the *ātman*, absolutely sole, although in truth one, appears manifold as the sun in diversified mirrors of water" (*Yā. Ya.* 3.144), "The sole *ātman* dwells in every being, as the moon reflects itself in [manifold stretches of] water. It is seen as One or as manifold [depending on the position of consciousness]" (*Amṛ.* 12), "In truth, as this *Vivasvat* [the Sun], which is light, although sole appears in a manifold way coming into contact with different waters, so this resplendent *ātman* without birth, through [contact with] the *upādhis* assumes a nature [apparently] diversified in various bodies."

And so [the *Brahmasūtra*] establishes definitively, also through various examples, that *Brahman* is only that which is devoid of qualifications. Nevertheless [on the part of a hypothetical opponent] a doubt again could be raised in these terms: "Instead, because it is not perceived that [the nature of the superimpositions, etc.] is similar to water, there is no correspondence [between this type of comparison and the *ātman*]" (*Bra. Sū.* 3.2.19).

According to such objection, the illustration mentioned would not be appropriate to the illustrated object since the *ātman*, being devoid of form and omnipresent, cannot result as established in places delimited by a form, similar to [the image] of the sun on the [surface of the various stretches of] water. So in the subsequent aphorism: "[Given that *Brahman*] is within [being the substrate of the formal manifestation], it appears to participate in growing and diminishing because of the similarity of both, it is so" (*Bra. Sū.* 3.2.20), [Bādarāyaṇa-Vyāsa makes comprehensible that], if we exclude only the part that is intended for discussion [and which consists in the analogy] between the illustrated object and the illustration, in fact nobody can prove that there is identity in every one of their aspects; if such an identity existed in every aspect, then the same relationship [of analogy] between the illustrated object and the illustration would not be there. Here what we would like to discuss is "the [apparent] participation in the increase and the decrease."

The image of the sun that is reflected on the water increases [in dimension] with the increase of the [dimension of the stretch of] water and decreases with the decrease [...] of the water, it moves when the water is moving and it divides when the water divides. In this way [the reflected image] is conforming to the contingent conditions of the water, while the sun does not really possess such a nature. Equally, although also *Brahman* is immutable and has sole nature and is always identical to itself, because of its reflecting itself within the *upādhis* like the body, etc., it appears to be taking the conditions of those limiting superimpositions, such as increasing or decreasing, etc. So, once that which is meant to be expounded is ascertained, [Bādarāyana-Vyāsa] sanctions the appriopriateness of the illustration in relation to the illustrated object.

Therefore, by reference to these and other similar passages: "He made the body [of the beings] with two feet and the body [...] with four feet. At first that Being, become bird, penetrated into the bodies" (*Bṛ.* II.V.18), "*Indra*, through the *māyā*, is perceived as of manifold form" (*Bṛ.* II.V.19), "The *Prakṛti* must be recognized, in truth, as the *māyā* and the great Lord, in truth, as He who governs the *māyā*" (*Śve.* IV.10), "The Possessor of the *māyā* manifests this universe" (*Śve.* IV.9), "...so the *ātman* internal to every being, although sole, takes every single form, remaining detached" (*Ka.* II.II.10), "A sole *Deva* is concealed in all beings" (*Śve.* VI.11), "That, cutting through this very top [of the head], penetrated through this opening" (*Ai.* I.III.12), "That one has penetrated [into these bodies] to the tip of the nails..." (*Bṛ.* I.IV.7), "Having created it, in that very same he penetrated" (*Tai.* II.VI.1), [Bādarāyana-Vyāsa] puts an end [to the discussion] with the aphorism: "And from the declaration [of the Scriptures]" (*Bra. Sū.* 3.2.21).

Thus, after having shown that the supreme *Brahman* can only be associated with the *upādhis* [through *avidyā*], he concludes that the *Brahman* is absolutely devoid of qualification, while the differentiation correlated to the limiting superimpositions is induced by the *māyā*, the way it happens for the sun [whose image is reflected] on the water.

Besides, also the direct experience of those who have realized *Brahman* refutes the universal unfolding [as reality]. They have effectively comprehended that awareness of the *ātman* is the only reality beyond the phenomenal universe. And in this sense [the *Śruti* together with the

Smṛti] describes the realization of those [knowers of the *Brahman* in the following and other passages]: "In this [state], when with the knowledge of the *ātman* [one] has become all the beings, what troubling, what affliction, [can there be] for he who recognizes himself as [supreme] unity?" (*Ī.* 7), "...there is nothing else that has to be recognized, having recognized all as *Brahman*" (*Śve.* I.12), "Such is the teaching concerning *nirvāṇa*" (*Sub.* XI.1), "There where, in truth, it is as if there were another, there one sees the other..." (*Bṛ.* IV.III.31), "But when, for him, all has become his very *ātman*, then by means of what and what could be seen?" (*Bṛ.* IV.V.15), "Also [a spiritual aspirant called] Nidāgha, having received the teaching of non-dualism, became devoted to it and as a result realized that all the beings were none else than the *ātman* itself. Therefore, realizing identity with *Brahman*, O 'Twice-born,' he attained the final liberation" (*Vi. Pu.* 2.16.19-20), "Certainly the one who, in truth, knows the supreme *Brahman* becomes the same *Brahman*..." (*Mu.* III.II.9).

In this way the reality of the manifold universe is refuted by both the *Śruti* and the *Smṛti*, through both reasoning and the experience [of those who have realized *Brahman*].

The things absolutely dissimilar and endowed with contrary attributes are often identified with one another [because of ignorance]. A sweet substance is considered sour, the [color] yellow [is mistaken] for white or vice-versa. At times to the incorporeal sky are associated [fallacious notions like those of] surface, impurity, etc. The same error of reciprocal superimposition is made between the body and the *ātman* [through *avidyā*]. The idea of the *ātman*, which is without form, is erroneously superimposed on what is not the *ātman* and has therefore a totally opposite nature, being endowed with form [as the body, etc.]. [That a person thinks]: "I am fat," "I am slim" is a common eperience. "If one who kills thinks of [really] killing and one who is killed thinks of being killed, both do not know: this [*ātman*] does not kill nor is it killed" (*Ka.* I.II.19), "The one who believes to be killed and the one who thinks to kill are both in error. That [the *ātman*] cannot kill nor be killed" (*Bha. Gī.* II.19), "All actions are urged by the *guṇas*; but he who is subjected to his [empirical] 'I' thinks: 'I am acting'" (*Bha. Gī.* III.27).

From passages like these drawn from the *Śruti* and the *Smṛti* it is seen that [because of ignorance] the characteristics of the *ātman* are superimposed on the non-*ātman* and vice versa. The [*Śvetāśvatara*] *Upaniṣad* expounds its teaching to remove this [false] superimposition, so that [the aspirant] can realize the knowledge of the non-dual *ātman*.

Notes

[1] The quotation drawn from the *Śatapatha Brāhmaṇa* refers to the four-monthly sacrifices (*caturmāsayavajña*), each of which is celebrated at the beginning of each season of four months, and which are known as: *Vaiśvadeva*, *Varuṇapraghāsa* and *Śākamedha*.

[2] With regard to the passage mentioned (*śloka* 11) of the *Īśa Upaniṣad*, it has to be borne in mind that "knowledge" (*vidyā*) and "non-knowledge" (*avidyā*) are not referring to the common meaning that these terms have in relation to *Advaita*, respectively "metaphysical knowledge" (*jñāna*) and "ignorance" (*ajñāna*). In the context of this *Upaniṣad*, non-knowledge–*avidyā* expresses what lies outside the simple cognitive act, therefore all that falls within the activity of ritual order (sacrificial rites, prayer, invocations) or within action of an ascetic nature (discipline, austerity, ethical prescriptions), etc.; while the knowledge-*vidyā* contains, as in other similar Texts, the meaning of formal "meditation" performed on the Divinities or on the Principles that support the manifestation. In this light it is clear that through non-knowledge as ritual activity, etc., the being enters the aspired-for subsequent existential conditions, while by means of knowledge, as meditation, the being attains identity with those universal Principles whose existence continues together with that of the manifestation. Therefore, only metaphysical knowledge in its purest sense (*jñāna*) involves attaining awareness of the Being in that it is and does not become: i.e., the identity with *Brahman*.

[3] Possible incomplete descriptions of meditations, rituals, etc., must be integrated, drawing also from other sections of the *Vedas*. Regarding this, refer to *Brahmasūtra* 3.3, with Śaṅkara's Commentary, *sūtras*: 1-8, 10, 19-22, 34, 59.

[4] "Fulfilling the [prescribed] *karman*, one can wish to live in the world for a hundred years. In this way, one is free from error; the individual [however] should not be a slave of *karman*."

The knower does not act with the sense of functioning as agent or to satisfy any desire, nor does he perform any action aiming at obtaining a fruit. The action—however devoid of the sense of being the agent—can be performed by him either under the influence of the latent impressions (*vāsanās*) responsible for his present birth or as spontaneous expression of Knowledge. For the knower, also, the very notion of individuality has ceased to be; therefore any possible action on his part appears as such and endowed with variations of fruit only from the perspective of the non-knower.

[5] The hypothetical opponent maintains that because the *ātman* is not known directly, while on the one hand objects like that expressed by the concept "you" and others are, as happens in common experience, and on the other hand the *ātman* itself has a nature quite different from that of any other definable thing, no superimposition on That is possible; as a consequence, not even the removal of such superimposition is possible. Therefore, according to the opponent, the condition of adherence or bondage to the cyclical becoming can in no way be eliminated.

[6] In reality the *ātman* represents an evidence as "content of the pure consciousness when it is freed from any superimposed attribute," therefore as undeniable and indisputable awareness of being. So, in theory, everybody possesses "cer-

tainty regarding the *ātman*." Nevertheless, the intellect of the individual who believes he is the subject of the action is darkened by the latent impressions (*vāsanās*) because of that fictitious identification and by those coming from the experience of the fruit. In this way, the original certitude of being the *ātman* is impeded, veiled by those mental contents. As a consequence, reality is attributed to objects that are simple modifications negating even the evidence of their non-being when these forms dissolve.

[7] The "double nature" (*rūpadvaya*) qualified-differentiated is that which belongs to the *upādhi*, and the unqualified-undifferentiated is that which belongs only to the ultimate Reality.

[8] Sentences that specifically deal with an object precisely as it is are called *tatpradhānas*, that is "having that [such object] as the principal and specific topic"; on the other hand, those sentences dealing with an object in a generic way together with other objects are called *atapradhānas*, that is "not having that as principal object." Obviously the first ones exercise a greater influence than the second ones with regard to the significance of their assertions.

SANSKRIT TEXT

śvetāśvataropaniṣadidaṁ vivaraṇamalpagranthaṁ brahmajijñāsūnāṁ sukhāvabodhāyārabhyate I citsadānandādvitīyabrahmasvarūpo 'pyātmā svāśrayayā svaviṣayayāvidyayā svānubhavagamyayā sābhāsayā pratibaddhasvābhāvikāśeṣapuruṣārthaḥ prāptāśeṣānartho 'vidyāparikalpitaireva sādhanairiṣṭaprāptiṁ cāpuruṣārthaṁ puruṣārthaṁ manyamāno mokṣārthamalabhamāno makarādibhiriva rāgādibhiritastataḥ samākṛṣyamāṇaḥ suranaratiryagādiprabhedabheditanānāyoniṣu saṁcarankenāpi sukṛtakarmaṇā brāhmaṇādyadhikāriśarīraṁ prāpta īśvarārthakarmānuṣṭhānenāpagatarāgādimalo 'nityatvādidarśanenotpannehāmutrārthabhogavirāga upetyācāryamācāryadvāreṇa vedāntaśravaṇādināhaṁ brahmāsmīti brahmātmatattvamavagamya nivṛttājñānatatkāryo vītaśoko bhavati I avidyānivṛttilakṣaṇasya mokṣasya vidyādhīnatvādyujyate ca tadarthopaniṣadārambhaḥ II tathā tadvijñānādamṛtatvam I "tamevaṁ vidvānamṛtaiha bhavati" (nṛ. 1.6) I "nānyaḥ panthāvidyate 'yanāya" (śve. 6.15) I "na cedihāvedīnmahatī vinaṣṭiḥ" (ke. 2.5) I "ya etadviduramṛtāste bhavanti" (bṛ. 4.4.14) I "kimicchankasya kāmāya śarīramanu sañjvaret" (bṛ. 4.4.12) I "taṁ viditvā na lipyate karmaṇā pāpakena" (bṛ. 4.4.23) I "tarati śokamātmavit" (chā. 7.1.3) I "nicāyya tanmṛtyumukhātpramucyate" (ka. 1.3.15) I "etadyo veda nihitaṁ guhāyāṁ so 'vidyāgranthiṁ vikiratīha somya" (mu. 2.1.10) I "bhidyate hṛdayagranthiśchidyante sarvasaṁśayāḥ I kṣīyante cāsya karmāṇi tasmindṛṣṭe parāvare" (mu . 2.2.8) I "yathā nadyaḥ syandamānāḥ samudre 'staṁ gacchanti nāmarūpe vihāya tathā vidvānnāmarūpādvimuktaḥ parātparaṁ puruṣ amupaiti divyam" (mu. 3.2.8) I "sa yo ha vai tatparamaṁ brahma veda brahmaiva bhavati" (mu. 3.2.9) I "sa yo ha vai tadacchāyamaśarīramalohitaṁ śubhramakṣaraṁ vedayate yastu somya" (pra. 4.10) I "sa sarvamavaiti" I "taṁ vedyaṁ puruṣaṁ veda yathā mā vo mṛtyuḥ parivyathāḥ" (pra. 6.6) I "tatra ko mohaḥ kaḥ śoka ekatvamanupaśyataḥ" (ī. 7) I "vidyayāmṛtamaśnute" (ī. 11) I "bhūteṣu bhūteṣu vicitya dhīrāḥ pretyāsmāllokādamṛtā bhavanti" (ke. 2.5) I "apahatya pāpmānamanante svarge loke jyeye pratitiṣṭhati" (ke. 4.9) I "tanmayā amṛtā vai babhūvuḥ" (śve. 5.6) I "tadvātmatattvaṁ prasamīkṣya dehī ekaḥ kṛtārtho bhavate vītaśokaḥ" (śve. 2.14) I "ya etadviduramṛtāste bhavanti" (bṛ. 4.4.14) I "īśaṁ taṁ jñātvāmṛtā bhavanti" (śve. 3.7) I "tadevopayanti I nicayyemāṁ śāntimatyantameti" (ka. 1.1.17) I "tamevaṁ jñātvā mṛtyupāśāṁśchinatti" (śve. 4.15) I "ye pūrvaṁ devā ṛṣayaśca taṁ viduḥ" (śve. 5.6) I "teṣāṁ śāntiḥ śāśvatī netareṣām" (ka. 2.2.13) I "buddhiyukto jahātīha ubhe sukṛtaduṣkṛte" (bha. gī. 2.50) I "karmajaṁ buddhiyuktā hi phalaṁ tyaktvā manīṣīṇaḥ I janmabandhavinirmuktāḥ padaṁ gacchantyanāmayam" (bha. gī. 2.51) I "sarvaṁ jñānaplavenaiva vṛjinaṁ saṁtariṣyasi I jñānāgniḥ sarvakarmāṇi bhasmasātkurute tathā" (bha. gī. 4.36-37) I "etadbuddhvā buddhimānsyātkṛtakṛtyaśca bhārata" (bha. gī. 15.20) I "tato māṁ tattvato jñātvā viśate tadanantaram" (bha. gī. 18.55) I "sarveṣāmapi caiteṣāmātmajñānaṁ paraṁ smṛtam I taddhyagryaṁ sarvavidyānāṁ prāpyate hyamṛtaṁ yataḥ I prāpyaitatkṛtakṛtyo hi dvijo bhavati nānyathā II evaṁ yaḥ sarvabhūteṣu paśyatyātmānamātmanā I sa sarvasamatāmetya brahmābhyeti sanātanam II samyagdarśanasampannaḥ karmabhirna nibadhyate I darśanena vihīnastu saṁsāraṁ pratipadyate" "karmaṇā badhyate janturvidyayā ca vimucyate I tasmātkarma na kurvanti yatayaḥ pāradarśinaḥ II jñānaṁ niḥśreyasaṁ prāhurvṛddhā niścayadarśinaḥ I tasmājjñānena śuddhena mucyate sarvapātakaiḥ" "evaṁ mṛtyuṁ jāyamānaṁ viditvā jñānena vidvāṁsteja abhyeti nityam I na vidyate hyanyathā tasya panthāstaṁ matvā kavirāste prasannaḥ" "kṣetrajñasyeśvarajñānādviśuddhiḥ paramā matā" "ayaṁ tu paramo dharmo yadyogenātmadarśanam" "ātmajñaḥ śokasaṁtīrṇo na bibheti kutaścana I mṛtyoḥ sakāśānmaraṇādathavānyakṛtādbhayāt" "na jāyate na mriyate na vadhyo na ca ghātakaḥ I na badhyo bandhakārī vā na mukto na ca mokṣadaḥ II puruṣaḥ paramātmā tu yadato 'nyadasacca tat" evaṁ śrutismṛtītihāsādiṣu jñānasyaiva mokṣasādhanatvāvagamādyujyata evopaniṣadārambhaḥ II kiṁcopaniṣatsamākhyayaiva jñānasyaiva paramapuruṣārthasādhanatvamavagamyate I tathā hi upaniṣadityupanipūrvasya saderviśaraṇagatyavasādanārthasya rūpamācakṣate I upaniṣacchabdena vyācikhyāsitagranthapratipādyavastu viṣayā vidyocyate I tādarthādgrantho 'pyupaniṣat I ye mumukṣ avo dṛṣṭānuśravikaviṣayavitṛṣṇāḥ santa upaniṣacchabditavidyāṁ tanniṣṭhatayā niścayena śīlayanti teṣāmavidyādeḥ saṁsārabījasya viśaraṇādvināśātparabrahmagamayitṛtvādgarbhajanmajarāmaraṇādyupadravāvasādayitṛtvādupaniṣatsamākhyayāpyanyakṛtātparaṁ śreya iti brahmavidyopaniṣaducyate ll nanu bhavedevamupaniṣadārambho yadi vijñānasyaiva mokṣasādhanatvaṁ bhavet l na caitadasti l karmaṇāmapi mokṣasādhanatvāvagamāt – "apāma somamamṛtā abhūma" "akṣayyaṁ ha vai cāturmāsyayājinaḥ sukṛtaṁ bhavati" ityādinā ll na tvetadasti śrutismṛtivirodhānnyāyavirodhācca l śrutivirodhastāvat – "tadyatheha karmajito lokaḥ kṣīyata evamevāmutra puṇyajito lokaḥ kṣīyate" (chā. 8.1.6) "tamevaṁ vidvānamṛta iha bhavati" (nṛ. 1.6) l "nānyaḥ panthā vidyate 'yanāya" (śve. 3.8, 6.15) l "na karmaṇā na prajayā dhanena tyāgenaike amṛtatvamānaśuḥ" (kai. 3) l "plavā hyete adṛḍhā yajñarūpā aṣṭādaśoktamavaraṁ yeṣu karma l etacchreyo ye 'bhinandanti mūḍhā jarāmṛtyuṁ te punarevāpiyanti" (mu. 1.2.7) l "nāstyakṛtaḥ kṛtena" (mu. 1.2.12) l "karmaṇā badhyate janturvidyayā ca vimucyate l tasmātkarma na kurvanti yatayaḥ pāradarśinaḥ" "ajñānamalapūrṇatvātpurāṇo malinaḥ smṛtaḥ l tatkṣayādvai bhavenmuktirnānyathā karmakoṭibhiḥ" "prajayā karmaṇā muktirdhanena ca satāṁ na hi l tyāgenaikena muktiḥ syāttadabhāve bhramantyāho" "karmodaye karmaphalānurāgāstathānuyanti na taranti mṛtyum" "jñānena vidvāṁsteja abhyeti nityaṁ na vidyate hyanyathā tasya panthāḥ" "evaṁ trayīdharmamanuprapannā gatāgataṁ kāmakāmā labhante" (bha. gī. 9.21) l "śramārthamāśramāścāpi varṇānāṁ paramārthataḥ" "āśramairna ca vedaiśca yajñaiḥ sāṁkhyairvrataistathā l ugraistapobhirvividhairdānairnānāvidhairapi l na labhante tamātmānaṁ labhante jñāninaḥ svayam" "trayīdharmamadharmārthaṁ kiṁpākaphalasaṁnibham l nāsti tāta sukhaṁ kiñcidatra duḥkhaśatākule ll tasmānmokṣāya yatatā kathaṁ sevyā mayā trayī" "ajñānapāśabaddhatvādamuktaḥ puruṣaḥ smṛtaḥ ll jñānāttasya nivṛttiḥ syātprakāśāttamaso yathā l tasmājjñānena muktiḥ syādajñānasya parikṣayāt" "vratāni dānāni tapāṁsi yajñāḥsatyaṁ ca tīrthāśramakarmayogāḥ l svargārthamevāśubhamadhruvaṁ ca jñānaṁ dhruvaṁ śāntikaraṁ mahārtham" "yajñairdevatvamāpnotitapobhirbrahmaṇaḥ padam l dānena vividhānbhogāñjñānānmokṣamavāpnuyāt" "dharmarajjvā vrajedūrdhvaṁ pāparajjvā vrajedadhaḥ l dvayaṁ jñānāsinā chittvā videhaḥ śāntimṛcchati" "tyaja dharmamadharmaṁ ca ubhe satyānṛte tyaja I ubhe satyānṛte tyaktvā yena tyajasi tattyaja" evaṁ śrutismṛtivirodhānna karmasādhanamamṛtatvaṁ nyāyavirodhācca I karmasādhanatve mokṣasya caturvidhakriyāntarbhāvādanityatvaṁ syāt I yatkṛtakaṁ tadanityamiti karmasādhyasya nityatvādarśanāt I nityaśca mokṣaḥ sarvavādibhirabhyupagamyate I tathā ca śrutiścaturmāsyaprakaraṇe – "prajāmanu prajāyase tadu te martyāmṛtam" iti I kiṁ ca sukṛtamiti sukṛtasyākṣayatvamucyate I sukṛtaśabdaśca karmaṇi II nanvevaṁ tarhi karmaṇāṁ devādiprāptihetutvena bandhahetutvameva II satyam I svato bandhahetutvameva I tathā ca śrutiḥ – "karmaṇā pitṛlokaḥ" (bṛ. 1.5.16) "sarva ete puṇ yalokā bhavanti" (chā. 2.23.1) "iṣṭāpūrtaṁ manyamānā variṣṭhaṁ nānyacchreyo vedayante pramūḍhāḥ I nākasya pṛṣṭhe te sukṛte 'nubhūtvemaṁ lokaṁ hīnataraṁ vā viśanti" (mu. 1.2.10) I "evaṁ karmasu niḥsrehā ye kecitpāradarśinaḥ I vidyāmayo 'yaṁ puruṣo na tu karmamayaḥ smṛtaḥ" (ma. bhā. ā. 51.32) "evaṁ trayīdharmamanuprapannā gatāgataṁ kāmakāmā labhante" (bha. gī. 9.21) iti I yadā punaḥ phalanirapekṣamīśvarārthaṁ karmānutiṣṭhanti tadā mokṣ asādhanajñānasādhanāntaḥkaraṇaśuddhisādhanapāramparyeṇa mokṣ asādhanaṁ bhavati I tathāha bhagavān – "brahmaṇyādhāya karmāṇi saṅgaṁ tyaktvā karoti yaḥ I lipyate na sa pāpena padmapatramivāmbhasā II kāyena manasā buddhyā kevalairindriyairapi I yoginaḥ karma kurvanti saṅgaṁ tyaktvātmaśuddhaye" (bha. gī. 5.10-11) I "yatkaroṣi yadaśnāsi yajjuhoṣi dadāsi yat I yattapasyasi kaunteya tatkuruṣva madarpaṇam II śubhāśubhaphalairevaṁ mokṣyase karmabandhanaiḥ I saṁnyāsayogayuktātmā vimukto māmupaiṣyasi" (bha. gī. 9.27.28) iti I tathā ca mokṣe kramaṁ śuddhyabhāve mokṣābhāvaṁ karmabhiśca tacchuddhiṁ darśayati śrīviṣṇudharme – "anūcānastato yajvā karmanyāsī tataḥ param I tato jñānitvamabhyeti yogī muktiṁ kramāllabhet" "anekajanmasaṁsāracite pāpasamuccaye I nākṣīṇe jāyate puṁsāṁ govindābhimukhī matiḥ" "janmāntarasahasreṣu tapojñānasamādhibhiḥ I narāṇāṁ kṣīṇapāpānāṁ kṛṣṇe bhaktiḥ prajāyate" "pāpakarmāśayo hyatra mahāmuktivirodhakṛt I tasyaiva śamane yatnaḥ kāryaḥ saṁsārabhīruṇā" "suvarṇādimahādānapuṇ yatīrthāvagāhanaiḥ I śārīraiśca mahākleśaiḥ śāstroktastacchamo bhavet" "devatāśrutisacchāstraśravaṇaiḥ puṇyadarśanaiḥ I guruśuśrūṣaṇ aiścaiva pāpabandhaḥ praśāmyati" yājñavalkyo śuddhyapekṣāṁ tatsādhanaṁ ca darśayati – "kartavyāśayaśuddhistu bhikṣukeṇa viśeṣataḥ I jñānotpattinimittatvātsvatantrīkaraṇāya ca" (yā. ya. 62) I malino hi yathādarśo rūpālokasya na kṣamaḥ I tathāvipakvakaraṇa ātmajñānasya na kṣamaḥ" (yā. ya. 1.4.1) I "ācāryopāsanaṁ vedaśāstrārthasya vivekitā I satkarmaṇāmanuṣṭhānaṁ saṅgaḥ sadbhirgiraḥ śubhāḥ II stryālokālambhavigamaḥ sarvabhūtātmadarśanam I tyāgaḥ parigrahāṇāṁ ca jīrṇakāṣāyadhāraṇam II viṣayendritasaṁrodhastandrālasyavivarjanam I śarīraparisaṁkhyānaṁ pravṛttiṣvaghadarśanam II nīrajastamasā sattvaśuddhirniḥspṛhatā śamaḥ I etairupāyaiḥ saṁśuddhasattvayogyamṛtī bhavet" (yā. ya. 156-189) I "yato vedāḥ purāṇāni vidyopaniṣadastathā I ślokāḥ sūtrāṇi bhāṣyāṇi yaccānyadvāṅmayaṁ kvacit II vedānuvacanaṁ yajño brahmacaryaṁ tapo damaḥ I śraddhopavāsaḥ svātantryamātmano jñānahetavaḥ" (yā. ya. 189-190) I tathā cātharvaṇe viśuddhyapekṣamātmajñānaṁ darśayati – "janmāntarasahasreṣu yadā kṣīṇāstu kilbiṣāḥ II tadā paśyanti yogena saṁsārocchedanaṁ mahat" (yo. 1.78-79) I "yasminviśuddhe viraje ca citte ya ātmavatpaśyanti yatayaḥ kṣīṇadoṣāḥ" "tametaṁ vedānuvacanena brāhmaṇā vividiṣanti yajñena dānenatapasānāśakena" (bṛ. 4.4.22) I iti Bṛhadāraṇyake vividiṣāhetutvaṁ yajñādīnāṁ darśayati II nanu "vidyāṁ cāvidyāṁ ca yastadvedobhayaṁ saha" (ī. 11) I "tapo vidyā ca viprasya naiḥśreyasakaraṁ param" ityādinā karmaṇāmapyamṛtatvaprāptihetutvamavagamyate II satyam I avagamyata eva tadapekṣitaśuddhidvāreṇa na ca sākṣāt I tathā hi – "vidyāṁ cāvidyāṁ ca" (ī. 11) "tapo vidyā ca viprasya naiḥśreyasakaraṁ param" ityādinā jñānakarmaṇorniḥśreyasahetutvamabhidhāya kathamanayostaddhetutvamityākāṅkṣāyāṁ "tapasā kalmaṣ aṁ hanti vidyayāmṛtamaśnute" "avidyayā mṛtyuṁ tīrtvā vidyayāmṛtamaśnute" (ī. 11) I iti vākyaśeṣeṇa karmaṇaḥ kalmaṣakṣayahetutvaṁ vidyāyā amṛtaprāptihetutvaṁ pradarśitam I yatra tu śuddhyādyavāntarakāryānupadeśastatrāpi śākhāntaropasaṁhāranyāyenopasaṁhāraḥ kartavyaḥ II nanu "kurvanneveha karmāṇi jijīviṣecchataṁsamāḥ" (ī. 2) iti yāvajjīvakarmānuṣṭhānaniyame sati kathaṁ vidyāyā mokṣasādhanatvam II ucyate – karmaṇyadhikṛtasyāyaṁ niyamo nānadhikṛtasyāniyojyasya brahmavādinaḥ I tathā ca viduṣ aḥ karmānadhikāraṁ darśayati śrutiḥ – "naitadvidvānṛṣiṇā vidheyo na rudhyate vidhinā śabdacāraḥ I etaddha sma vai tatpūrve vidvāṁso 'gnihotraṁ na juhavāñcakrire" "etaṁ vai tamātmānaṁ viditvā brāhmaṇāḥ putraiṣaṇāyāśca vittaiṣaṇāyāśca lokaiṣaṇāyāśca vyutthāyātha bhikṣācāryaṁ caranti" (bṛ. 3.5.1) । "etaddha sma vai tadvidvāṁsa āhurṛṣayaḥ kāvaṣeyāḥ kimarthā vayamadhyeṣyāmahe kimarthā vayaṁ yakṣyāmahe" "sa brāhmaṇaḥ kena syādyena syāttenedṛśa eveti" yathāha bhagavān – "yastvātmaratireva syādātmatṛptaśca mānavaḥ । ātmanyeva ca saṁtuṣṭastasya kāryaṁ na vidyate ॥ naiva tasya kṛtenārtho nākṛteneha kaścana । na cāsya sarvabhūteṣu kaścidarthavyapāśrayaḥ" (bha. gī. 3.17-18) । tathā cāha bhagavānparameśvaro laiṅge kālakūṭopākhyāne – "jñānenaitena viprasya tyaktasaṅgasya dehinaḥ । kartavyaṁ nāsti viprendrā asti cettattvavinna ca ॥ iha loke pare caiva kartavyaṁ nāsti tasya vai । jīvanmukto yatastu syādbrahmavitparamārthataḥ ॥ jñānābhyāsarato nityaṁ virakto hyarthavitsvayam । kartavyabhāvamutsṛjya jñānamevādhigacchati ॥ varṇāśramābhimānī yastyaktvā jñānaṁ dvijottamāḥ । anyatra ramate mūḍhaḥ so 'jñānī nātra saṁśayaḥ ॥ krodho bhayaṁ tathā lobho moho bhedo madastamaḥ । dharmādharmau ca teṣāṁ hi tadvaśācca tanugrahaḥ ॥ śarīre sati vai kleśaḥ so 'vidyāṁ saṁtyajettataḥ । avidyāṁ vidyayā hitvā sthitasyaiveha yoginaḥ ॥ krodhādyā nāśāmāyānti dharmādharmau ca naśyataḥ । tatkṣayācca śarīreṇa na punaḥ saṁprayujyate ॥ sa eva muktaḥ saṁsārādduḥkhatrayavivarjitaḥ" tathā śivadharmottare – "jñānāmṛtena tṛptasya kṛtakṛtyasya yoginaḥ । naivāsti kiñcitkartavyamasti cenna sa tattvavit ॥ lokadvaye 'pi kartavyaṁ kiñcidasya na vidyate । ihaiva sa vimuktaḥ syātsampūrṇaḥ samadarśanaḥ" । tasmādviduṣaḥ kartavyābhāvādavidyāvadviṣaya evāyaṁ kurvannevetyādikarmaniyamaḥ । kurvanneveti ca nāyaṁ karmaniyamaḥ kiṁ tu vidyāmāhātmyaṁ darśayituṁ yathākāmaṁ karmānuṣṭhānameva draṣṭavyam । etaduktaṁ bhavati – yāvajjīvaṁ yathākāmaṁ puṇyapāpādikaṁ kurvatyapi viduṣi na karmalepo bhavati vidyāsāmarthyāditi । tathā hi – "īśāvāsyamidaṁ sarvam" (ī. 1) । ityārabhya "tena tyaktena bhuñjīthāḥ" (ī. 1) iti viduṣaḥ sarvakarmatyāgenātmapālanamuktvāniyojyo brahmavidi tyāgakartavyatoktirapyayuktaivokteti matvā cakitaḥ sanvedo viduṣastyāgakartavyatāmapi noktavān । kurvanneveha loke vidyamānaṁ puṇyapāpādikaṁ karma yāvajjīvaṁ jijīviṣet । na puṇyādibandhabhayātpuṇyādikaṁ tyaktvā tūṣṇīmavatiṣṭheta । evaṁ tāvatkarmāṇi kurvatyapi viduṣi tvayīto yāvajjīvānuṣṭhānādanyathābhāvaḥ svarūpātpracyutiḥ puṇyādinimittasaṁsārānvayo nāsti I athavetaḥ karmānuṣṭhānottarakālabhāvyanyathābhāvaḥ saṁsārānvayo nāsti I yasmāttvayi vinyastaṁ na karma lipyate I tathā ca śrutyantaram – "na lipyate karmaṇā pāpakena" (bṛ. 4.4.23) I "evaṁvidi pāpaṁ karma na śliṣyate" (chā. 4.14.3) I "nainaṁ kṛtākṛte tapataḥ" (bṛ. 4.4.22) I "evaṁ hāsya sarve pāpmānaḥ pradūyante" (chā. 5.24.3) I "jñānāgniḥ sarvakarmāṇi bhasmasātkurute tathā II laiṅge – jñāninaḥ sarvakarmāṇi jīryante nātra saṁśayaḥ I krīḍannapi na lipyeta pāpairnānāvidhairapi" I śivadharmottare 'pi – "tasmājjñānāsinā tūrṇamaśeṣaṁ karmabandhanam I kāmākāmakṛtaṁ chittvā I śuddhaścātmani tiṣṭhati II yathā vahnirmahāndīptaḥ śuṣkamārdraṁ ca nirdahet I tathā śubhāśubhaṁ karma jñānāgnirdahate kṣaṇāt II padmapatraṁ tathā toyaiḥ svasthairapi na lipyate I śabdādiviṣayāmbhobhistadvajjñānī na lipyate II yadvanmantrabalopetaḥ krīḍansarpairna daṁśyate I krīḍannapi na lipyate tadvadindriyapannagaiḥ II mantrauṣadhibalairyadvajjīryate bhakṣitaṁ viṣam I tadvatsarvaṇi pāpāni jīryante jñāninaḥ kṣaṇāt" tathā ca sūtrakāraḥ – "puruṣārtho 'taḥ śabdāditi bādarayaṇaḥ" (bra. sū. 3.4.1) iti jñānasyaiva paramapuruṣārthahetutvamabhidhāya "śeṣatvātpuruṣārthavādo yathā" (bra. sū. 3.4.2) ityādinā karmāpekṣitakartṛpratipādakatvena vidyāyāḥ karmaśeṣatvamāśaṅkya "adhikopadeśāttu bādarayaṇasya" (bra. sū. 3.4.8) ityādinā kartṛtvādisaṁsāradharmarahitāpahatapāpmādirūpabrahmopadeśāttadvijñānapūrvikāṁ tu karmādhikārasiddhiṁ tvāśāsānasya karmādhikārahetoḥ kriyākārakaphalalakṣaṇasya samastasya prapañcasyāvidyākṛtasya vidyāsāmarthyātsvarūpopamardadarśanātkarmādhikārocchittiprasaṅgādbhinnaprakaraṇatvādbhinnakāryatvācca parasparavikalpaḥ samuccayo 'ṅgāṅgibhāvo vā nāstīti pratipadya "ata eva cāgnīndhanādyanapekṣā" (bra. sū. 3.4.25) iti vidyāyā eva paramapuruṣārthahetutvādagnīndhanādyāśramakarmāṇi vidyāyāḥ svārthasiddhau nāpekṣitavyānīti pūrvoktasyādhikaraṇasya phalamupasaṁhṛtyātyantamevānapekṣāyāṁ prāptāyāṁ "sarvāpekṣā ca yajñādiśrutyeraśvavat" (bra. sū. 3.4.26) iti nātyantamanapekṣā I utpannā hi vidyā phalasiddhiṁ prati na kiñcidanyadapekṣate I utpattiṁ pratyapekṣata eva I "vividiṣanti yajñena" iti śruteriti vividiṣāsādhanatvena karmaṇāmupayogaṁ darśitavān I tathā ca "nāviśeṣāt" (bra. sū. 3.4.13) "stutaye 'numatirvā" (bra. sū. 3.4.14) iti sūtradvayena kurvannevetimantrasyāvidvadviṣayatvena vidyāstutitvena cārthadvayaṁ darśitavān I ata uktena prakāreṇa jñānasyaiva mokṣasādhanatvādyuktaḥ paropaniṣadārambhaḥ II nanu bandhasya mithyātve sati jñānanivartyatvena jñānādamṛtatvaṁ syāt I na tvetadasti I pratipannatvādbādhābhāvādyuṣmadādisvarūpatvenātmano vilakṣaṇatve sādṛśyādyabhāvādadhyāsāsambhavācca II ucyate – na tāvatpratipannatvena satyatvaṁ vaktuṁ śakyate pratipatteḥ satyatvamithyātvayoḥ samānatvāt I nāpi bādhābhāvātsatyatvam I vidhimukhena kāraṇamukhena ca bādhasambhavāt I tathāhi śrutiḥ – prapañcasya mithyātvaṁ māyākāraṇatvaṁ ca darśayati "na tu taddvitīyamasti" (bṛ. 4.3.23) "ekatvam" "nāsti dvaitam" "kuto vidite vedyaṁ nāsti" "ekamevādvitīyam" (chā. 6.2.1) I "vācārambhaṇaṁ vikāro nāmadheyam" (chā. 6.1.4) I "ekameva sat" "neha nānāsti kiñcana" (bṛ. 4.4.19) I "ekadhaivānudraṣṭavyam" (bṛ. 4.4.20) I "māyāṁ tu prakṛtiṁ vidyāt" (śve. 4.10) I "māyī sṛjate viśvametat" (śve. 4.9) I "indro māyābhiḥ pururūpa īyate" (bṛ. 2.5.19) ityādibhirvākyaiḥ II "ajo 'pi sannavyayātmā bhūtānāmīśvaro 'pi san I prakṛtiṁ svāmadhiṣṭhāya sambhavāmyātmamāyayā" (bha. gī. 4.6) I "avibhaktaṁ ca bhūteṣu vibhaktamiva ca sthitam" (bha. gī. 13.16) I tathā ca brāhme purāṇe – "dharmādharmau janmamṛtyū sukhaduḥkheṣu kalpanā I varṇāśramāstathā vāsaḥ svarge naraka eva ca II puruṣasya na santyete paramārthasya kutracit I dṛśyate ca jagadrūpamasatyaṁ satyavanmṛṣā II toyavanmṛgatṛṣṇā tu yathā marumarīcikā I raupyavatkīkasaṁ bhūtaṁ kīkasaṁ śuktireva ca II sarpavadrajjukhaṇḍaśca niśāyāṁ veśmamadhyagaḥ I eka evendurdvau vyomni timirāhatacakṣuṣaḥ II ākāśasya ghanībhāvo nīlatvaṁ snigdhatā tathā I ekaśca sūryo bahudhā jalādhāreṣu dṛśyate II ābhāti paramātmāpi sarvopādhiṣu saṁsthitaḥ I dvaitabhrāntiravidyākhyā vikalpo na ca tattathā II paratra bandhāgāraḥ syātteṣāmātmābhimāninām I ātmabhāvanayā bhrāntyā dehaṁ bhāvayatāṁ sadā II āprajñamādimadhyāntairbhramabhūtaistribhiḥ sadā I jāgratsvapnasuṣuptaistu cchāditaṁ viśvataijasam II svamāyayā svamātmānaṁ mohayeddvaitarūpayā I guhāgataṁ svamātmānaṁ labhate ca svayaṁ harim II vyomni vajrānalajvālākalāpo vividhākṛtiḥ I ābhāti viṣṇoḥ sṛṣṭiśca svabhāvo dvaitavistaraḥ II śānte manasi śāntaśca ghore mūḍhe ca tādṛśaḥ I īśvaro dṛśyate nityaṁ sarvatra na tu tattvataḥ ll lohamṛtpiṇḍahemnāṁ ca vikāro na ca vidyate l carācarāṇāṁ bhūtānāṁ dvaitatā na ca satyataḥ ll sarvago tu nirādhāre caitanyātmani saṁsthitā l avidyā dviguṇāṁ sṛṣṭiṁ karotyātmāvalambanāt ll sarpasya rajjutā nāsti nāsti rajjau bhujaṅgatā l utpattināśayornāsti kāraṇaṁ jagato 'pi ca ll lokānāṁ vyavahārārthamavidyeyaṁ vinirmitā l eṣā vimohinītyuktā dvaitādvaitasvarūpiṇī ll advaitaṁ bhāvayedbrahma sakalaṁ niṣkalaṁ sadā l ātmajñaḥ śokasaṁtīrṇo na bibheti kutaścana ll mṛtyoḥ sakāśānmaraṇādathavānyakṛtādbhayāt l na jāyate na mriyate na vadhyo na ca ghātakaḥ ll na baddho bandhakārī vā na mukto na ca mokṣ adaḥ l puruṣaḥ paramātmā tu yadato 'nyadasacca tat ll evaṁ buddhvā jagadrūpaṁ viṣṇormāyāmayaṁ mṛṣā bhogāsaṅgādbhavenmuktastyaktvā sarvavikalpanām ll tyaktasarvavikalpaśca svātmasthaṁ niścalaṁ manaḥ l kṛtvā śānto bhavedyogī dagdhendhana ivānalaḥ ll eṣā caturviṁśatibhedabhinnā māyā parā prakṛtistatsamutthau l kāmakrodhau lobhamohau bhayaṁ ca viṣādaśokau ca vikalpajālam ll dharmādharmau sukhaduḥkhe ca sṛṣṭirvināśapākau narake gatiśca l vāsaḥ svarge jātayaścāśramāśca rāgadveṣau vividhā vyādhayaśca ll kaumāratāruṇyajarāviyogasaṁyogabhogānaśanavratāni l itīdamīdṛgvidayaṁ nidhāya tūṣṇīmāsīnaḥ sumatiṁ vividdhi" tathā ca śrīviṣṇudharme ṣaḍadhyāyyām – "anādisambandhavatyā kṣetrajño 'yamavidyayā l yuktaḥ paśyati bhedena brahmatattvātmani sthitam ll paśyatyātmānamanyacca yāvadvai paramātmanaḥ l tāvatsaṁbhrāmyate janturmohito nijakarmaṇā ll saṁkṣīṇāśeṣakarmā tu paraṁ brahma prapaśyati l abhedenātmanaḥ śuddhaṁ śuddhatvādakṣayo bhavet ll avidyā ca kriyāḥ sarvā vidyā jñānaṁ pracakṣate l karmaṇā jāyate janturvidyayā ca vimucyate ll advaitaṁ paramārtho hi dvaitaṁ tadbhinna ucyate l paśutiryaṅmanuṣyākhyaṁ tathaiva nṛpa nārakam ll caturvidho 'pi bhedo 'yaṁ mithyājñānanibandhanaḥ l ahamanyo 'paraścāyamamī cātra tathāpare ll ajñānametaddvaitākhyamadvaitaṁ śrūyatāṁ param l mama tvahamiti prajñāviyuktamavikalpavat ll avikāryamanākhyeyamadvaitamanubhūyate l manovṛttimayaṁ dvaitamadvaitaṁ paramārthataḥ ll manaso vṛttayastasmāddharmādharmanimittajāḥ l niroddhavyāstannirodhe dvaitaṁ naivopapadyate ll manodṛṣṭamidaṁ sarvaṁ yatkiñcitsacarācaram l manaso hyamanībhāve 'dvaitabhāvaṁ tadāpnuyāt ll karmaṇāṁ bhāvanā yeyaṁ sā brahmaparipanthinī I karmabhāvanayā tulyaṁ vijñānamupajāyate II tādṛgbhavati vijñāptiryādṛśī khalu bhāvanā I kṣaye tasyāḥ paraṁ brahma svayameva prakāśate II parātmanormanuṣyendra vibhāgo 'jñānakalpitaḥ I kṣaye tasyātmaparayoravibhāgo 'ta eva hi II ātmā kṣetrajñasaṁjño hi saṁyuktaḥ prākṛtairguṇaiḥ I taireva vigataḥ śuddhaḥ paramātmā nigadyate" tathā ca śrīviṣṇupurāṇe – "paramātmā tvamevaiko nānyo 'sti jagataḥ pate I tavaiṣa mahimā yena vyāptametaccarācaram II yadetaddṛśyate mūrtametajjñānātmanastava I bhrāntijñānena paśyanti jagadrūpamayoginaḥ II jñānasvarūpamakhilaṁ jagadetadabuddhayaḥ I arthasvarūpaṁ paśyanto bhrāmyante mohasaṁplave II ye tu jñānavidaḥ śuddhacetasaste 'khilaṁ jagat I jñānātmakaṁ prapaśyanti tvadrūpaṁ pārameśvaram" (1.4.38-41) "ahaṁ hariḥ sarvamidaṁ janārdano nānyattataḥ kāraṇakāryajātam I īdṛṅmano yasya na tasya bhūyo bhavodbhavā dvandvagadā bhavanti" (1.22.87) I "jñānasvarūpamatyantaṁ nirmalaṁ paramārthataḥ I tadevārthasvarūpeṇa bhrāntidarśanataḥ sthitam" (1.2.6) I "jñānasvarūpo bhagavānyato 'sāvaśeṣamūrtirna tu vastubhūtaḥ I tato hi śailābdhidharādibhedāñjānīhi vijñānavijṛmbhitāni" (2.12.39) I "vastvasti kiṁ kutracidādimadhyaparyantahīnaṁ satataikarūpam I yaccānyathātvaṁ dvija yāti bhūmau na tattathā tatra kuto hi tattvam II mahī ghaṭatvaṁ ghaṭataḥ kapālikā kapālikācūrṇarajastato 'ṇuḥ I janaiḥ svakarmastimitātmaniścayairālakṣyate brūhi kimatra vastu II tasmānna vijñānamṛte 'sti kiñcitkvacitkadāciddvija vastujātam vijñānamekaṁ nijakarmabhedavibhinnacittairbahudhābhyupetam II jñānaṁ viśuddhaṁ vimalaṁ viśokamaśeṣalobhādinirastamaṅgam I ekaṁ sadaikaṁ paramaḥ pareśaḥ sa vāsudevo na yato 'nyadasti II sadbhāva evaṁ bhavato mayokto jñānaṁ tathā satyamasatyamanyat I etattu yatsaṁvyavahārabhūtaṁ tatrāpi coktaṁ bhuvanāśritaṁ te" (2.12.41-45) I "avidyāsaṁcitaṁ karma taccāśeṣeṣu jantuṣu II ātmā śuddho 'kṣaraḥ śānto nirguṇaḥ prakṛteḥ paraḥ I pravṛddhyapacayau na sta ekasyākhilajantuṣu" (2.13.70-71) "yattu kālāntareṇāpi nānyasaṁjñāmupaiti vai I pariṇāmādisambhūtāṁ tadvastu nṛpa tacca kim" (2.13.100) I "yadyanyo 'sti paraḥ ko 'pi mattaḥ pārthivasattama I tadaiṣo 'hamayaṁ cānyo vaktumevamapīṣyate II yadā samastadeheṣu pumānhyeko vyavasthitaḥ I tadā hi ko bhavānso 'hamityetadvipralambhanam II tvaṁ rājā śibikā ceyaṁ vayaṁ vāhāḥ puraḥsarāḥ | ayaṁ ca bhavato loko na sadetattvayocyate" (2.13.90-92) | "vastu rājeti yalloke yacca rājabhaṭātmakam | tathānye ca nṛpatvaṁ ca tattatsaṅkalpanāmayam" (2.13.99) | "anāśī paramārthaśca prājñairabhyupagamyate" (2.14.24) | "paramārthastu bhūpāla saṁkṣ epācchrūyatāṁ mama || eko vyāpī samaḥ śuddho nirguṇaḥ prakṛteḥ paraḥ | janmavṛddhyādirahita ātmā sarvagato 'vyayaḥ || parajñānamayaḥ sadbhirnāmajātyādibhiḥ prabhuḥ | na yogavānna yukto 'bhūnnaiva pārthiva yokṣyate || tasyātmaparadeheṣu saṁyogo hyeka eva yat | vijñānaṁ paramārtho 'sau dvaitino 'tathyadarśinaḥ" (2.14.28-31) | "evamekamidaṁ vidvannabhedi sakalaṁ jagat | vāsudevābhidheyasya svarūpaṁ paramātmanaḥ" (2.15.35) | "nidāgho 'pyupadeśena tenādvaitaparo 'bhavat || sarvabhūtānyabhedena sa dadarśa tadātmanaḥ | tathā brahma tato muktimavāpa paramāṁ dvija || sitanīlādibhedena yathaikaṁ dṛśyate nabhaḥ | bhrāntadṛṣṭibhirātmāpi tathaikaḥ saṁpṛthakpṛthak" (2.16.19-20) | "ekaḥ samastaṁ yadihāsti kiñcittadacyuto nāsti paraṁ tato 'nyat | so 'haṁ sa ca tvaṁ sa ca sarvametadātmasvarūpaṁ tyaja bhedamoham || itīritastena sa rājavaryastattyāja bhedaṁ paramārthadṛṣṭiḥ | sa cāpi jātismaraṇāptabodhastatraiva janmanyapavargamāpa" (2.16.22-24) | tathā laiṅge – "tasmādajñānamūlo hi saṁsāraḥ sarvadehinām | paratantre svatantre ca bhidābhāvādvicārataḥ || ekatvamapi nāstyeva dvaitaṁ tatra kuto 'styaho | ekaṁ nāstyatha martyaṁ ca kuto mṛtasamudbhavaḥ || nāntaḥprajño bahiṣprajño na cobhayatha eva ca | na prajñānaghanastvevaṁ na prājño 'prajña eva saḥ || vidite nāsti vedyaṁ ca nirvāṇaṁ paramārthataḥ | ajñānatimirātsarvaṁ nātra kāryā vicāraṇā || jñānaṁ ca bandhanaṁ caiva mokṣo nāpyātmano dvijāḥ | na hyeṣā prakṛtirjīvo vikṛtiśca vikārataḥ | vikāro naiva māyaiṣā sadasadvyaktivarjitā" tathāha bhagavānparāśaraḥ – "asmāddhi jāyate viśvamatraiva pravilīyate | sa māyī māyayā baddhaḥ karoti vividhāstanūḥ || na cātraivaṁ saṁsarati na ca saṁsārayetparam | na kartā naiva bhoktā ca na ca prakṛtipūruṣau || na māyā naiva ca prāṇaścaitanyaṁ paramārthataḥ | tasmādajñānamūlo hi saṁsāraḥ sarvadehinām || nityaḥ sarvagato hyātmā kūṭastho doṣavarjitaḥ | ekaḥ sa bhidyate śaktyā māyayā na svabhāvataḥ || tasmādadvaitamevāhurmunayaḥ paramārthataḥ | jñānasvarūpamevāhurjagadetadvicakṣaṇāḥ || arthasvarūpamajñānātpaśyantyanye kudṛṣṭayaḥ | kūṭastho nirguṇo vyāpī caitanyātmā svabhāvataḥ ǁ dṛśyate hyartharūpeṇa puruṣairbhrāntidṛṣṭibhiḥ । yadā paśyati cātmānaṁ kevalaṁ paramārthataḥ ǁ māyāmātramidaṁ dvaitaṁ tadā bhavati nirvṛtaḥ । tasmādvijñānamevāsti na prapañco na saṁsṛtiḥ" evaṁ śrutyādinā nāmādikāraṇopanyāsamukhena svarūpeṇa ca bādhitatvātprapañcasya mithyātvamavagamyate । asthūlādilakṣaṇasya brahmaṇastadviparītasthūlākāro mithyā bhavitumarhati । yathaikasya candramasastadviparītadvitīyākārastadvat ǁ tathā ca sūtrakāro "na sthānato 'pi parasyobhayaliṅgaṁ sarvatra hi" (bra. sū. 3.2.11) iti svarūpata upādhitaśca viruddha rūpadvayāsambhavānnirviśeṣameva brahmetyupapādya "na bhedāt" (bra. sū. 3.2.12) iti bhedaśrutibalātkimiti saviśeṣ amapi brahma nābhyupagamyata ityāśaṅkya "na pratyekamatadvacanāt" ityupādhibhedasya śrutyaiva bādhitatvādabhedaśrutibalātsaviśeṣasya grahaṇāyogānnirviśeṣamevetyupapādya "api caivameke" (bra. sū. 3.2.13) iti bhedanindāpūrvakamabhedamevaike śākhinaḥ samāmananti – "manasaivedamāptavyam । neha nānāsti kiñcana । mṛtyoḥ sa mṛtyumāpnoti ya iha nāneva paśyati" (bṛ. 4.4.19, ka. 4.10-11) । "ekadhaivānudraṣṭavyamiti" (bṛ. 4.4.20) । "bhoktā bhogyaṁ preritāraṁ ca matvā sarvaṁ proktaṁ trividhaṁ brahmametat" (śve. 1.12) iti sarvabhogyabhoktṛniyantṛlakṣaṇasya prapañcasya brahmaikasvabhāvatābhidhīyata iti ǁ punarapi nirviśeṣapakṣe dṛḍhīkṛte kimityekasvarūpasya ubhayasvarūpāsambhave 'nākārameva brahmāvadhāryate na punarviparītamityāśaṅkya "arūpavadeva hi tatpradhānatvāt" (bra. sū. 3.2.14) iti । rūpādyākārarahitameva brahmāvadhārayitavyam । kasmāt । tatpradhānatvāt । "asthūlamanaṇ vahrasvamadīrgham" (bṛ. 3.8.8) । "aśabdamasparśamarūpamavyayam" (ka. 1.3.15) । "ākāśo vai nāma nāmarūpayornirvahitā te yadantarā tadbrahma" (chā. 8.14.1) । "tadetadbrahmāpūrvamanaparamanantaramabāhyamayamātmā brahma sarvānubhūrityetadanuśāsanam" (bṛ. 2.5.19) ityevamādīni niṣprapañcabrahmātmatattvapradhānāni । itarāṇi kāraṇabrahmaviṣayāṇi na tatpradhānāni । tatpradhānānyatatpradhānebhyo balīyāṁsi bhavanti । atastatparaśrutipratipannatvānnirviśeṣameva brahmāvagantavyaṁ na punaḥ saviśeṣamiti । nirviśeṣ apakṣamupapādya kā tarhyākāravadviṣayāṇāṁ śrutīnāṁ gatiḥ । ityākāṅkṣāyāṁ "prakāśavaccāvaiyarthyāt" (bra. sū. 3.2.15) iti candrasūryādīnāṁ jalādyupādhikṛtanānātvavacca brahmaṇo 'pyupādhikṛtanānātvarūpasya vidyamānatvāttadākāravato brahmaṇa ākāraviśeṣ opadeśa upāsanārtho na virudhyate ‖ evamavaiyarthyaṁ nānākāra-brahmaviṣayānāṁ vākyānāmiti । bhedaśrutīnāmaupādhikabrahmaviṣ ayatvenāvaiyarthyamuktvā punarapi nirviśeṣameva brahmeti draḍha-yitum "āha ca tanmātram" (bra. sū. 3.2.16) iti "sa yathā saindha-vaghano 'nantaro 'bāhyaḥ kṛtsno rasaghana eva । evaṁ vā are 'yamātmānantaro 'bāhyaḥ kṛtsnaḥ prajñānaghana eva" (bṛ. 4.5.13) iti śrutyupanyāsena vijñānavyatiriktarūpāntarābhāvamupanyasya "darśayati cātho api smaryate" (bra. sū. 3.2.17) iti । "athāta ādeśo neti neti" (bṛ. 2.3.6) । "anyadeva tadviditādatho aviditādadhi" (ke. 1.3) । "yato vāco nivartante 'prāpya manasā saha" (tai. 2.4.1) ‖ "pratyastamitabhedaṁ yatsattāmātramagocaram । vacasāmātmasaṁ-vedyaṁ tajjñānaṁ brahmasaṁjñitam" "viśvasvarūpavairūpyaṁ lakṣaṇ aṁ paramātmanaḥ" ityādiśrutismṛtyupanyāsamukhena pratyastami-tabhedameva brahmetyupapādya "ata eva copamā sūryakādivat" (bra. sū. 3.2.18) iti । yata eva caitanyamātrarūpo neti netyātmako viditāviditābhyāmanyo vācāmagocaraḥ pratyastamitabhedo viśva-svarūpavilakṣaṇasvarūpaḥ paramātmāvidyopādhiko bhedaḥ । ata eva cāsyopādhinimittāmapāramārthikīṁ viśeṣavattāmabhipretya jalasū-ryādirivetyupamā dīyate mokṣaśāstreṣu "ākāśamekaṁ hi yathā ghaṭādiṣu pṛthkapṛthak । tathātmaiko hyanekaśca jalādhāreṣvivāṁ-śumān" (yā. ya. 3.144) । "eka eva tu bhūtātmā bhūte bhūte vya-vasthitaḥ । ekadhā bahudhā caiva dṛśyate jalacandravat" "yathā hyayaṁ jyotirātmā vivasvānapo bhinnā bahudhaiko 'nugacchan । upādhinā kriyate bhedarūpo devaḥ kṣetreṣvevamajo 'yamātmā" iti dṛṣṭāntabalenāpi nirviśeṣameva brahmetyupapādya "ambuvadagrahaṇ āt" (bra. sū. 3.2.19) ityātmano 'mūrtatvena sarvagatatvena jalasū-ryādivanmūrtasaṁbhinnadeśasthitatvābhāvāddṛṣṭāntadārṣṭāntikayoḥ sādṛśyaṁ nāstītyāśaṅkya "vṛddhihrāsabhāktvam" (bra. sū. 3.2.20) iti na hi dṛṣṭāntadārṣṭāntikayorvivakṣitāṁśamuktvā sarvasārūpyaṁ kenaciddarśayituṁ śakyate । sarvasārūpye dṛṣṭāntadārṣṭāntikabhāvo-ccheda eva syāt । vṛddhihrāsabhāktvamatra vivakṣitam । jalagata-sūryapratibimbaṁ jalavṛddhau vardhate jalahrāse ca hrasati jalaca-lane calati jalabhede bhidyata ityevaṁ jaladharmānuvidhāyi bha-vati na tu paramārthataḥ sūryasya tattvamasti । evaṁ paramārtha-to 'vikṛtamekarūpamapi sadbrahma dehādyupādhyantarbhāvādbhajata evopādhidharmānvṛddhihrāsādīniti I vivakṣitāṁśapratipādanena dṛṣṭāntadārṣṭāntikayoḥ sāmañjasyamuktvā "darśanācca" (bra. sū. 3.2.21) iti "puraścakre dvipadaḥ puraścakre catuṣpadaḥ puraḥ sa pakṣī bhūtvā puraḥ puruṣa āviśat" (bṛ. 2.5.18) I "indro māyābhiḥ pururūpa īryate" (bṛ. 2.5.19) I "māyāṁ tu prakṛtiṁ vidyānmāyinaṁ tu maheśvaram" (śve. 4.10) I "māyī sṛjate viśvametam" (śve. 4.9) I "ekastathā sarvabhūtāntarātmā rūpaṁ rūpaṁ pratirūpo bahiśca" (ka. 2.2.9-10) I "eko devaḥ sarvabhūteṣu gūḍhaḥ" (śve. 6.11) I "sa etameva sīmānaṁ vidāryaitayā dvārā prāpadyata" (ai. 1.3.12) I "sa eṣa iha praviṣṭa ānakhāgrebhyaḥ" (bṛ. 1.4.7) I "tatsṛṣṭvā tadevānuprāviśat" (tai. 2.6.1) ityādinā parasyaiva brahmaṇa upādhiyogaṁ darśayitvā nirviśeṣameva brahma I bhedastu jalasūryādivadaupādhiko māyānibandhana ityupasaṁhṛtavān II kiñca brahmavidāmanubhavo 'pi prapañcasya bādhakaḥ I teṣāṁ niṣprapañcātmadarśanasya vidyamānatvāt I tathā hi teṣāmanubhavaṁ darśayati I "yasminsarvāṇi bhūtāni ātmaivābhūdvijānataḥ I tatra ko mohaḥ kaḥ śoka ekatvamanupaśyataḥ" (ī. 7) I "vidite vedyaṁ nāsti" iti I evaṁ nirvāṇamanuśāsanam I "yatra vā anyadiva syāttatrānyo 'nyatpaśyet" (bṛ. 4.3.31) I "yatra tvasya sarvamātmaivābhūttatkena kaṁ paśyet" (bṛ. 4.5.15) I "yadetaddṛśyate mūrtametajjñānātmanastava I bhrāntijñānena paśyanti jagadrūpamayoginaḥ" (vi. pu. 1.4.38) II "ye tu jñānavidaḥ śuddhacetasaste 'khilaṁ jagat I jñānātmakaṁ prapaśyanti tvadrūpaṁ pārameśvaram" (vi. pu. 1.4.41) I "nidāgho 'pyupadeśena tenādvaitaparo 'bhavat II sarvabhūtānyaśeṣeṇa dadarśa sa tadātmanaḥ I tathā brahma tato muktimavāpa paramāṁ dvija" (vi. pu. 2.16.19-20) I "atrātmavyatirekeṇa dvitīyaṁ yo na paśyati I brahmabhūtaḥ sa eveha vedaśāstra udāhṛtaḥ" ityevaṁ śrutismṛtiyuktito 'nubhavataśca prapañcasya bādhitatvādatyantavilakṣaṇānāmasadṛśarūpāṇāṁ madhuratiktaśvetapītādīnāmapi parasparādhyāsadarśanādamūrte 'pyākāśe jalamalinatādyadhyāsadarśanādātmānātmanoratyantavilakṣaṇayormūrtāmūrtayorapi tathā sambhavātsthūlo 'haṁ kṛśo 'hamiti dehātmanoradhyāsānubhavāt I "hantā cenmanyate hantuṁ hataścenmanyate hatam I ubhau tau na vijānīto nāyaṁ hanti na hanyate" (ka. 1.2.19-20) I ityādiśrutidarśanāt "ya enaṁ hantāram" (bha. gī. 2.19) I "prakṛteḥ kriyamāṇāni" (bha. gī. 3.27) itismṛtidarśanāccādhyāsasya prahāṇāyātmaikatvavidyāpratipattaya upaniṣadārabhyate II

GLOSSARY

Note

The words in the glossary, transliterated from Sanskrit, follow the standard English alphabetical order. For simplicity, both short and long vowels are presented under one letter, and the three sibilants (*ś*, *ṣ*, *s*) appear under the letter *s*.

Abbreviations: m = masculine noun, f = feminine noun, n = neuter noun, N = name or proper noun, adj. = adjective, adv. = adverb, pro. = pronoun; n/m, for example, although grammatically masculine, indicates a neuter concept.

abhāva (m): Non-existence, non-being. Opposite of *bhāva*.

adharma (m): Not in conformity with the *dharma*; that which violates the universal Order or the Law (*dharma*).

adhyāsa (m): Superimposition, substitution. For Śaṅkara: "Appearance in a given place of something that is known from elsewhere, on the basis of imaginative projection."

adhyātman (n/m): The *paramātman* (supreme Self), *ātman* as Principle, or primordial *ātman*. The intimate *ātman* (Self) of all beings.

adhyātmavidyā (f): The Knowledge of the first principles or of the universal or primordial *ātman* (Self). Supreme Knowledge.

adṛṣṭa (adj., n): The "not seen," the invisible. Principle non-perceived and non-perceivable by any faculty.

advaita (n): Non-duality, absence of duality. (adj.): Without-a-second.

Advaita Vedānta or *advaitavedānta*: The non-dual *Vedānta*, codified by Gauḍapāda and Śaṅkara. Metaphysical *darśana* (perspective) that transcends dualism (*dvaita*) as well as monism (*aikya*).

advaitavāda (m): Metaphysical doctrine of Non-duality formulated by Gauḍapāda and Śaṅkara.

advaitin (m): One who follows the *advaitavāda*, he who has realized Non-duality.

āgāminkarman (n): One of the three types of *karma*. It is the *karma* that will unfold in the future and, like the *saṁcitakarma*, it can be avoided. See *karma*.

Agni (N/m): The Vedic god of Fire. It also represents the sacred Fire evoked through asceticism and discipline.

agnihotra (n): Rite of daily oblation (*hotra*) to Agni, at dawn and after sunset.

aham (pro.): nominative singular "I," notion of "I" as individualized reflection of consciousness, proceeding from the *ātman* (Self) through the mediation of the incarnate reflection of consciousness (*jīva*). Prototype of the *ahaṁkara* or "sense of ego."

ahaṁkāra (m): Literally "what makes up the ego," or the "sense of the empirical ego." It constitutes consciousness in the individual state.

ahiṁsā (f): "Non-violence." It is one of the five *yamas* or prohibitions in Patañjali's *Yogasūtra* and constitutes a fundamental precept in Buddhism and Jainism.

ajāti (f): Non-generation.

ajātivāda (m): The doctrine of "non-generation" presented by Gauḍapāda in his *Kārikā* (verse commentary) to the *Māṇḍūkya Upaniṣad.*

ajñāna (n): Ignorance of metaphysical order (see also *avidyā*).

ākāśa (m, n): The "space," the universal ether that pervades the entire universe. It is the first of the five elements (*bhūta*), its characteristic being *śabda* (sound). Ether as quintessence of the Elements: fire, water and so on.

ānanda (n/m): Absolute beatitude, pure happiness, joy without objects. Condition that inheres to the awareness of the fullness of one's Being. One of the three inseparable and consubstantial aspects of *jīvātman* (Self): *sat, cit, ānanda.*

ānandamaya (adj.): Made or constituted (*maya*) of *ānanda* (beatitude).

ānandamayakośa (m): The sheath of beatitude. The innermost and subjective "casing." The seat of the *jīvā* in the deep sleep state. As it is determined as *kośa* (layer, sheath), it is already in the plane of limitations and therefore does not represent the *ānanda* of *Brahman.*

anātman or *anātma* (m/n): That which is not *ātman*. The non-Self or *ahaṁkāra*, the empirical ego.

aṅga (n): Body, means; constitutive element of a discipline or a state.

annamaya (adj.): Made or constituted (*maya*) of food (*anna*).

annamayakośa (m): The sheath of food. The outermost sheath of the *ātman* (Self). Gross sheath. It corresponds to the gross physical vehicle, made up in fact of food, transformed and assimilated.

antaḥkaraṇa (n): The internal organ, the "mind" in its full extension and various *vṛtti* (modifications), which includes: *buddhi* (intellect, intuitive perception or direct discernment), *ahaṁkāra* (sense of self), *citta* (projecting memory, deposit of subconscious tendencies and predispositions) and *manas* (empirical selective mind).

apara (adj./adv.): Inferior, lesser; non supreme, relative.

aparigraha (m): Non-possessiveness. One of the five *yamas* of Patañjali's *rāja yoga* or *yogadarśana*.

aparokṣa (adj.): Direct, immediate.

Aparokṣānubhūti (f): "The direct realization of the Self."

āraṁbhavāda (m): Evolutionary theory of dualism.

Āraṇyaka (m): The "Treaty of the forest (*araṇya*)." Transition texts that are among the *Brāhmaṇa* and the *Upaniṣads*.

artha (m): Generic meaning: object, good, function, purpose. One of the four goals of existence.

aśabda (adj.): Without sound. Referring to the silent *Brahma*, *Brahma nirguṇa* (without attributes); therefore beyond word-sound.

āsana (n): Position, posture of *haṭha yoga*. Third step or means of Patañjali's *rāja yoga*.

asat (n): Non-being; non-reality, that which is not nor exists in absolute.

asparśa (adj., n): "Without contact," without relation, without support, absolute.

asparśavāda (m): The doctrine of "without contact," of non-relation, expounded by Gauḍapāda in the *Māṇḍūkyakārikā*.

asparśayoga (m): The *yoga* of "without contact," the *yoga* of pure consciousness as the non-mediated realization of the *ātman* (Self).

asparśin (m): One who has realized the *asparśayoga*, also one who follows the *asparśavāda*.

āśrama (m): Hermitage, life stage. The four life stages in the traditional Hindu society are: *brahmacarya* (celibacy and study), *gṛhasthya* (social and family responsibility), *vānaprasthya* (hermit stage), *saṁnyāsa* (total renunciation). States of consciousness that determine the corresponding life stages.

asteya (n): Non-appropriation. One of the five *yama* of Patañjali's *rāja yoga*.

Atharva Veda (m): One of the four *Vedas*.

Ātmabodha (m): Consciousness of the *ātman*, knowledge of the Self, title of one of Śaṅkara's treatises (*prakaraṇa*) considered as fundamental for the knowledge of *Advaita Vedānta*.

ātmadhyāna (n): "Meditation on the *ātman*."

ātman (n/m): Self, Spirit, pure Consciousness, ontological "I." The *Ātman* is the absolute in us, completely outside of time-space-cause, and as such is identical to *Brahman*. Absolute in itself.

AUM (m): The sacred syllable OM (*oṁkāra*) in its constituent elements. It symbolizes the Absolute; see OM.

avasthātraya (n): The three "states": waking-gross (*viraṭ*), dream-subtle (*hiraṇyagarbha*), deep sleep-causal (*Īśvara*), on which *Vedānta* leads its investigation-discernment (*viveka*) to attain to the ultimate Reality or Fourth (*Turīya*).

avasthātrayasākṣin (m): Witness of the three states; *ātman* (Self), pure Consciousness without modifications.

avidyā (f): Metaphysical ignorance, ignorance with regard to the Reality, the noumenon, or the nature of Being. It is the individualized aspect of the universal ignorance, or *māyā*.

āvṛti (f): Veiling. Also *āvaraṇa*.

avṛtiśakti (f): The "veiling power" of *māyā-avidyā*.

avyakta (n): The undifferentiated, non-manifested condition of the Principle, universal One, undifferentiated condition of *prakṛti*-substance before it manifests.

Bādarāyaṇa (N): According to the Tradition, founder of *Vedānta* and author of the *Brahmasūtra*; often identified with Vyāsa.

Bhagavadgītā (f): "The Song of Bhagavan," "The Song of the Blessed One"; philosophical and religious poem that is part of *Bhışmaparvan*, the sixth book of the *Mahābhārata*.

bhakta (m): Devout. One who follows the path of *bhakti* (devotion). Person full of love for the Divine.

bhakti (f): Ardent devotion, love for the Divine. Participation in the divine Being to the attainment of perfect union with It. For Śaṅkara, *bhakti* is "the constant search for one's real nature." We have *aparabhakti* (non-supreme *bhakti*) and *parabhakti* (supreme *bhakti*).

bhaktiyoga (m): The *yoga* of devotion. The *sādhanā* rests on filling the emotional body with love so as to cause "breaking through the level" that is necessary to attain the union with the Beloved.

bhāva (m): Birth, phenomenal existence.

bhūta (n): The existent, constituting substance, primordial element. First elements of nature. The five sensible elements out of which all bodies are made: earth, water, fire, air, ether (*ākāśa*).

bodha (m): Intuitive knowledge, knowledge in that consciousness.

Brahmā (m): One of the three aspects of the Hindu *trimūrti* or the threefold form with which the qualified Being, *Brahman saguṇa* or *Īśvara*, manifests. It is the manifesting principle of the universe that corresponds to the creator aspect, in relation with the conservator (*Viṣṇu*) and the transforming one (*Śiva*).

brahmacārin (m): Person living the celibate and student *āśrama* (stage of life).

brahmacarya (n): The first of the four traditional *āśramas* (stages of life), that of *brahmacārin* (celibate and student).

brahmaloka (m): The celestial world, or the world of *Brahmā*.

Brahman or *Brahma* (n): The absolute Reality, the Absolute in itself. "That" (*Tat*), which is totally transcendent and unconditioned, always identical to itself. One-without-a-second.

Brahman nirguṇa or *nirguṇabrahma* (n): Non-qualified Reality, free (*nir*) of *guṇas* (attributes), absolute. It is applied to the absolute Brahman; see also Brahman.

Brahman saguṇa or *saguṇabrahma* (n): Qualified Being, with *guṇas* (attributes). First qualification of *nirguṇabrahman*; see also *Īśvara*.

brāhmaṇa (n): First of the four traditional social orders (*varṇas*), the sacredotal one who retains the knowledge of *Brāhman*. Liturgical exegesis texts annexed to the *vedas*.

Brahmasūtra (n): Aphorisms that constitute the basic text of *Vedānta*. Attributed to Bādarāyaṇa (or Vyāsa), in which he codified the main passages of the *Veda Upaniṣad*.

brahmavidyā (f): Knowledge of the Absolute, synonymous with *brahmajñāna*.

Bṛhadāraṇyaka Upaniṣad (f): The "*Upaniṣad* of the great Āraṇyaka," one of the oldest and most important Vedic *Upaniṣads*. It contains the *mahāvākya* (great aphorism) "*aham brahmāsmi*: I am *Brahman*."

buddhi (f): Superior intellect, discerning intelligence, pure reason, intuition of the universal.

buddhimayakośa: See *vijñānamayakośa*.

caitanya (n): Consciousness. Spirit. Absolute pure Intelligence.

cakra (n): "Wheel," "center." The various *cakras* represent determinations of the energy-awareness, or *śakti*.

cit (n): Pure and Absolute Consciousness (*caitanya*), pure Awareness, pure Intelligence, pure Knowledge. *Cit* is beyond any representative and cognitive process, beyond the mental and even beyond pure intellection or intellectual intuition (*buddhi*); yet it gives life to the mind itself, it provides support to its modifications and its functioning. One of the three inseparable and consubstantial aspects of *jivātman* (Self): *sat*, *cit*, *ānanda*.

citta (n): Mental substance through which *cit* condenses. Instrument of the mind through which the *jīva* materializes its individual world by giving "form" to the ideas and by making associations between them. One of the four faculties of the *antaḥkaraṇa* (internal organ), besides *buddhi, manas* and *ahaṁkāra*. Also contains memory impressions (*vāsanās*) and tendencies or mental seeds (*saṁskāras*).

dama (m): self-control; control of the mind; control of the various organs and body sensations.

darśana (n): Occasion in which to contemplate a Sage. "Perspective." The term is used in relation to the doctrine of the *Veda* and to the six orthodox schools of Hindu traditional philosophy. The six schools are: *Sāṁkhya*, *Yoga*, *Vaiśeṣika*, *Nyāya*, *Pūrva Mīmānsā* and *Uttara Mīmānsā* or *Vedānta*.

dehasaṁnyāsa (m): The complete renunciation of the body without giving up sustaining it.

deśa (m): Space.

deva (m): "One who is resplendent," angelic being, Deity.

dhāraṇā (f): Concentration. The sixth step of Patañjali's *rāja yoga*.

dharma (m): Stems from the root *dhṛ*, which indicates supporting, preserving, "wearing." It designates in general terms a "way of being," i.e., the essential nature of a being, therefore conformity with the Principle in accordance with the universal law of Equilibrium-Harmony. In metaphysical terms, that through which Harmony manifests as expression of the Unity of Being. In the individual order it relates to the action that one will be able to perform in accordance with the Principle (*karmadharma*), to attain liberation. The fundamental *dharma* of each human being is to become aware of and to realize in practice one's own divine Nature, which permeates all beings.

dhyāna (n): Meditation. The seventh step of of Patañjali's *rāja yoga*.

Dṛgdṛśyaviveka (m): Discernment between *ātman* (the spectator) and non-*ātman* (the spectacle). Title of a work, fundamental for the comprehension of *Advaita Vedānta*, attributed to Śaṅkara.

dṛk (m): The seer, the spectator, he who sees, perceives (*draṣṭṛ*).

dṛksthiti (f): "Firmness of vision," steadiness.

dṛśya (adj.): The visible, the object of vision or knowledge. The "spectacle" of which *ātman* is the "spectator" or witness.

dvaita (n, adj.): Duality, dualism; dualistic school; dual.

ens (n; Latin): Integral being, impersonal individuality, universal being, divine Person, supreme Being.

Gauḍapāda (N): Master of the *advaitavedānta*, of which he was the first codifier. Śaṅkara's spiritual Master. Author of the *Māṇḍūkya-kārikā* (or *Gauḍapādakārikā*), verse commentary to the *Māṇḍūkya Upaniṣad*, where the *ajātivāda* (doctrine of non-generation, non-creation) and the *asparśayoga* (*yoga* of no support) are expounded.

gṛhastha (m): The second of the traditional *āśramas* (stages of life). He who lives the state of head of family; the state of who fullfills his responsibilities.

guṇa (m): Attribute of *prakṛti*-substance or qualitative principle of the universal substance that is at the base of manifestation. "Constituent quality."

guru (m): Instructor, spiritual Teacher (*ācārya*), one who removes (*ru* stands for removing) ignorance (*gu* stands for obscurity or ignorance). Instructor in the *vedas*, performing purifying ceremonies.

haṭhayoga (m): *Yoga* of physiological well-being, aiming at perfection and control of the body for its transformation into the Temple of the Spirit.

Hiraṇyagarbha (m): "Golden germ," cosmic egg (*brahmāṇḍa*). The second of the three states of Being. The totality of the subtle universal manifestation, which comprehends its individual corresponding subtle aspect (*taijasa*).

indriya (n): Literally "power," indicates both the faculty of the senses and their corporeal organs. Together they constitute an instrument of knowledge (*jñānendriya*) and of action (*karmendriya*). The internal modification of the mind associated with the sensory organ itself.

Īśvara (m): "Divine Person," it represents what we could define as the personified God. It is the first determination of the absolute *Brahman*, and it comprehends the entire field of manifestation: gross, subtle and causal, from both the cosmic and individual points of view.

Itihāsa (m): Epic poems. The most important are the *Rāmāyaṇa* and the *Mahābhārata*.

jāgrat (n): Waking state. The other ones are: *svapna* or dream state, *suṣupti* or dreamless sleep state and *Turīya*, which transcends them all.

Jaimini (N): Codifier of the *Pūrva Mīmāṁsā*.

Jīva (m): Living being (*jīvin*), individualized Soul, reflection of consciousness of the *ātman* on the universal plane. It produces movement and activity within itself and engenders, through *ahaṁkāra*, the subject (Self-*aham*) as well as the object (world-*idam*) of experience, of knowledge.

jīvanmukta (adj.): "Liberated during life," one who has extinguished the threefold Fire.

jīvanmukti (f): "Liberation in life."

jīvātman (m): The *ātman* reflected in the *jīva*, Soul.

jñāna (n): Knowledge, from *jñā* (to know), identical to the Greek *gnosis*. Cathartic, liberating knowledge. Also one of the qualities of the Lord (*Bhagavad*): wisdom, intelligence.

jñānayoga (m): The yoga of Knowledge. Reintegration (*yoga*) into the Absolute actualized though knowledge-awareness; the pure metaphysical "way." The means are *viveka* (intuitive discernment) and *vairāgya* (detachment).

jñānin (m): Knower, one who practices the *Jñānayoga*, realized being.

kaivalya (n): Total and complete "isolation" from the threefold world. Independence from all things, total detachment. The state of absolute isolation from the non-Self that is realized by the pure *jñānin*.

kāla (m): Time, the internal dynamism that presents itself as succession. Designation of *Śiva*.

kalpa (adj., n): Cycle of time extending between two *pralayas* (cosmic dissolutions).

kāma (m): Desire, coveting, greed, attachment to the sensory world.

kāmamanas (n): Mental condition of complete conformity with desire; relationship between desire and empirical mind; emotion that proceeds from imagination. It is the characteristic of *manomayakośa*.

Kapila (N): Compiler of the *Sāṁkhya darśana* who lived in the VI century B.C.

karaṇa (n): Organ, instrument, means.

kāraṇa (n): Cause, origin.

kārikā (f): Commentary in verse.

karman (n): Action, activity, principle of causality, effects resulting from an action; rite. It is the inertia of the mental mass of the subject, which pushes him to act, think, identify and be in a specific condition. It can be considered as "cause" and as "effect" of the action, which forces the being into *saṁsāra* (perennial becoming).

karma yoga (m): *Yoga* of "action without action." Spiritual path that consists in acting in this world without attachment to the fruits of the work.

karmakāṇḍa (n): "Section on ritual action" of *Brāhmaṇa* texts.

kevala (adj., m): "Absolute," pure, whole. Generally refers to *Brahman* or to the *ātman,* that is, to the *jīvamukta*, which itself is isolated from the cycle of existential becoming and from the *māyā*-conforming movement. See *kaivalya*.

kevalin (m): One who has attained the state of *kaivalya* or *kevala*.

kośa (m): Shell, envelope, sheath, energetic sheath. According to *Vedānta,* five sheaths envelop the Self: *ānandamayakośa*, *vijñānamayakośa*, *manomayakośa*, *prāṇamayakośa* and *annamayakośa*.

kṣatriya (m): He who belongs to the regal-military order, to the order of the judges and the politicians, he who supports law and justice; one of the four traditional social orders (*varṇas*); it corresponds to the guardians of Plato's *Politéia*. cf. *Bhagavadgītā*.

kumbhaka (m): The state of retention of breath.

kuṇḍalinī (adj.): Literally the "rolled up." Serpentine force; nervous and psychical force placed in the lotus at the base of the spine (*mūlādhāracakra*).

laya (m): Dissolution-transformation, destruction, absorption (see *Pralaya*).

liṅga (n): Subtle character, reason. Phallus as symbol of energy. Its elliptic form with its two poles represents the Dyad, the bipolarity expressed in creation.

liṅgaśarīra (n): The subtle body made up of sheaths: *prāṇamaya*, *manomaya*, and *vijñānamaya*.

loka (m): "World." Cosmos, not to be viewed in a strictly spatial sense. Condition of existence as determined by the state of consciousness-knowledge.

lokāyata (m): Materialist doctrine promulgated by the Cārvāka school that posits gross matter as the foundation of the universe. Also, the materialists who follow the Cārvāka school.

māhāt (n): The "Great"; cosmic Intelligence; the great Mind. Principle of the cosmic manifestation according to the *Sāṁkhya darśana*. First effect of *mūlaprakṛti*.

mahāvākya (m): Great aphorism; the Vedic great aphorisms in which the *Vedānta* Doctrine is synthesized. The main *mahāvākyas* are four: *aham brahmāsmi*, I am *Brahman* (*Bṛhadāraṇyaka Upaniṣad* I.IV.10; of the "black" *Yajur Veda*); *tat tvam asi*, That thou art (*Chāndogya Upaniṣad* VI.VII.7; of the *Sāma Veda*); *prajñānaṁ brahma*, Brahman is pure consciousness (*Aitareya Upaniśad* V.3; of the *Ṛg Veda*); *ayam ātmā brahma*, This *ātman* is *Brahman* (*Māṇḍūkya Upaniṣad* II; of the *Atharva Veda*). The *mahāvākyas* must be meditated upon in the light of supraconscious intuition (*buddhi*) and not be the object of rational analysis of the empirical mind (*manas*).

manas (n): Mind, internal sense, individualized empirical mind endowed with rational-analytical ability, imaginative mind.

Māṇḍūkya Upaniṣad (n): *Upaniṣad* of the *Atharva Veda*, which synthesizes the teachings of *Advaita Vedānta*.

manomayakośa (m): The sheath constituted by the empirical mind, selective-instinctual mind that operates through attraction-repulsion. In it, the sense of ego (*ahaṁkāra*) is active.

mantra (m): Section of the *Vedas*, power words or sounds, hymns used in ritual acts, sacred word, formulae or verses expressed or meditated upon during concentration and meditation, vibrating thought.

manvantara (m): Period of Manu, cosmic cycle that comprehends four *yugas*: *satya*, *tretā*, *dvāpara*, *kali*.

maṭha or *maṭh* (m): Sacred place, monastery, cenoby.

mātrā (f): "Measure"; metric quantity; length of each foot (*pāda*), in the sense of paragraph, division, part.

mauna (n): The "all-encompassing silence" of the *Muni*.

maya (adj.): Particle meaning "made of," "constituted by."

māyā (f): Metaphysical ignorance, the world of names and forms as vital phenomenon; all that is modification superimposed (*upādhi*) on the pure Consciousness of the Self; "conformed movement," *Īśvara's* "sleep dream."

Mīmāṁsā (f): Literally, "deep reflection." The term refers, generally, to the in-depth study of the *Vedas* in order to determine the exact meaning of the *Śruti* and to draw the implicit consequences both in practice and in the intellectual sphere. It includes the last two of the six *darṣanas*, which are called *Pūrva Mīmāṁsā* or *Karma Mīmāṁsā*, and *Uttara Mīmāṁsā* or *Vedānta*.

mokṣa (m): Liberation, the attainment of eternal Beatitude as outcome of the recognition of the ultimate Truth; deliverance from ignorance (*avidyā*) from relativity-becoming and from all that constitutes *māyā* as the superimposed modification on the pure Consciousness of the *ātman*; the last of the four *puruṣārthas*.

mukti (f): Liberation, a synonym for *mokṣa*.

mūlabandha (m): Absorption of consciousness in its own origin. "Radical contraction," *haṭhayoga* practice that is associated with some *āsanas*, especially with the *prāṇāyāma* retention (*kumbhaka*), both internal and external. One of the fifteen steps described by Śaṅkāra in the *Aparokṣānubhūti*.

mumukṣutā or *mumukṣutva* (f, n): Intense aspiration for delivery from all bondage; longing for liberation as result of maturity of consciousness. In the *Vedānta* path, it is one of the four necessary means to penetrate the world of causes and to break the chain of superimpositions that veil Reality.

muni (m): Ascetic person practicing silence. One who knows the value of silence (*mauna*). State of consciousness of one who has realized the non-qualified Absolute.

nāman (n): Name; complementary to *rūpa*, form. According to *Vedānta*, that which has a name and also a form, and vice versa. The dyad *nāmarūpa* is what makes the differentiated and individualized being emerge from the substratum of unqualified Being. As Śaṅkara states, *nāma-rūpa* are mere mental modifications.

nāmarūpa (n): "Name-form." The world of names and of forms that constitute becoming; constitutive elements; elements that constitute and characterize individuality.

neti neti: "Not this, not this." Aphorism of negation through which the *jñānayogin* successively discards all that is appearance as relative and transitory, and through discernment (*viveka*) and detachment (*vairāgya*) attains *Brahman*, the permanent and absolute Substratum.

nirguṇa (adj.): Free from *guṇas*, non-qualified, absolute; it is applied to *Brahman*.

nirguṇabrahma (n, m): See *Brahman nirguṇa*.

nirvāṇa (n): Extinction, solution. Also *nivṛtti*. Supreme state in which the *jīva* has resolved into the non-dual *ātman*.

nirvikalpa (adj.): Free from differentiation, immutable, absolute, transcendent. The contrary is *savikalpa*.

nirvikalpasamādhi (m): *Samādhi* free from differentiations. Consciousness totally free from differentiations and, therefore, from duality.

niyama (m): Observances. The second step or means (*aṅga*) of the *rāja yoga* of Patañjali. The observances are: purity, contentment, burning aspiration, study and abandon to the Lord.

non-*ātman* (m): See *anātman*.

Nyāya (n): One of the six *darṣanas*, whose compiler was Gautama. The meaning of the term *nyāya* is "logic" or "method," "analytic investigation."

OM: The sacred syllable among all. Symbol of the Absolute, of *Brahman* and also of all the concepts the human being has of the Supreme, the Divine. This syllable is part of almost all *mantras*. The symbol itself is the symbol of Totality and of absolute Unity (non-duality) and is regarded as sacred in all of India. The syllable OM (*oṁkāra*) is seed of meditation, as well as its parts A, U, M, which express the gross, subtle and causal planes respectively. OM with "sound" represents the qualified Being, *Brahman saguṇa*, while the "silent" OM represents the non-qualified Being or *Brahman nirguṇa*.

pāda (m, n): "Foot" in the sense of paragraph, division, part. "Measure," in rhythmical poetry.

para (adj.): Other, different; superior, supreme.

paramātman (n): The Supreme *ātman* (Self), which is identical to *Brahman*; supreme Spirit.

Parāśara (N): Name of a *Ṛṣi*; the author, according to Tradition, of some *hymns* of the *Ṛg Veda*.

paravidyā (f): Supreme Knowledge, science of the Greater Mysteries, metaphysical Knowledge.

pariṇāmavāda (m): The *Sāṁkhya* doctrine by which primordial *prakṛti* is transformed in twenty-three principles, through which the principial causative Cause transforms itself into the effect (manifestation). To the *prakṛti* is contraposed the transcendent *puruṣa*, which remains in itself and with itself.

Patañjali (N): Codifier of *darśana Yoga*. His *Yogasūtra* constitute the basis of *rāja yoga* or regal *yoga*.

prajñā (f): Faculty to know, pure intellect (*buddhi*), knowledge (*jñāna*) pure knowledge, consciousness-awareness. Discriminative intelligence (*viveka*).

prājña (m): Causal body of the human *jīva*. In *prājña*, multiplicity and duality are reintegrated into unity of undifferentiated consciousness, as synthesis of knowledge. It also represents the *jīva* in the deep sleep state (*suṣupti*). It is the causal place of the *jīva*.

prakaraṇagrantha (m): "Specific treaties."

prakṛti (f): Nature, universal substance, *natura naturans*, the substance by which all sensible and intelligible forms are made. For *Vedānta* it is the equivalent of *māyā*, *pradhāna* or *avyakta*.

pralaya (m): Dissolution; return into undifferentiated state; dissolution of the manifestation, at the end of a "day" of *Brahmā* (*kalpa*).

prāṇa (m): Vital breath, cosmic breath, vital energy.

prāṇamayakośa (m): Sheath of the vital energy. It is constituted by the subtle energies that keep the gross body alive and active.

prāṇasaṁyama (n): "Control of vital energy."

praṇava (m): "That which is pronounced." The sacred syllable OM.

prāṇāyāma (m): "Control" of *prāṇa*, the pranic breathing through which we are able to control the breath. The fourth step (*aṅga*) in the *rāja yoga* of Patañjali. As *prāṇa* has different meanings, so *prāṇāyāma* can have different interpretations.

prārabdhakarman (n): Result or effect of past actions (*sāmcitakarman)* that have reached maturation (*prārabdha*), and which cannot be neutralized. See *sāmcitakarman* and *āgāminkarman*.

prasthānatraya (n): Threefold Testimony. The threefold Science of *Vedānta* constituted by the classical *Upaniṣads*, the *Brahmasūtra* and the *Bhagavadgītā*.

pratyāhāra (m): Abstraction. "Withdrawal" of the awareness from identification with sensory, energetic, perceptive, lower mental activities. The fifth step in the *rāja yoga* of Patañjali. It leads to the achievement of introspection, in which the mind detaches from the suggestion of external impressions and turns toward itself.

pūraka (m): The phase of inhalation, "breathing in," in *prāṇāyāma*.

Purāṇa (adj., N/n): Ancient, primordial. "Mythological collection." Sacred texts very popular in India. The *Purāṇa*, together with the *Itihāsa*, the *Āgama*, etc., form the *Smṛti*, or "recollected tradition"; of a human order.

puruṣa (m): Being, man, person, Self, Spirit. For *Sāṁkhya*, it is the positive principle-pole correlated to *prakṛti* or negative principle-pole. With its pure presence it stimulates *prakṛti's* activity. In union with *prakṛti* it stimulates the world. So *prakṛti* manifests the dynamism inherent in *puruṣa's* immobility.

Puruṣa Sūkta (n): "Hymn to *Puruṣa*," *Ṛg Veda* (X.90).

puruṣottama (m): Supreme *Puruṣa*, the universal Spirit. "The highest *Puruṣa*," assimilated to the supreme *Brahman* or *paramātma*.

Pūrvamīmāṁsā (N/f): The first *Mīmāṁsā*, also called *Karma Mīmāṁsā* or *Dharma Mīmāṁsā* because it concerns the sphere of action. It is one of the six orthodox *darśanas*; Jaimini was its compiler. Interior, endogenous searching.

rajas (n): One of the three *guṇas* (the other two being *tamas* and *sattva*), corresponding to activity, energy, desire, fire, passion, and responding to expansion, dynamic movement and development. In the hierarchical order of manifestation, *rajas* corresponds to the subtle plane, *tamas* to the gross and *sattva* to the causal plane.

rājayoga (m): The regal *Yoga*. Codified by Patañjali in his *Yogasūtra* and comprising eight steps.

recaka (m): The phase of exhalation, "breathing out," in *prāṇayāma*.

Ṛg Veda (N/m): "The *Veda* of Hymns." The first and oldest among the four *Vedas*.

ṛṣi (m): Seer. The great Sages who "heard" the *śruti* (Tradition) and handed it down through the *Vedas* and the *Upaniṣads*. In the *Śatapatha Brāhmaṇa* (XIV.5.2.6) are listed the following: Marīci, Atri, Aṅgiras, Pulaha, Kratu, Pulastya and Vasiṣṭha. The expression "The *ṛṣis* said" is tantamount to saying "So it is said in the Sacred Texts."

rūpa (n): Grace, beauty, splendor; nature, character, peculiarity; form, quality, essence; color; forms through which life manifests. See *nāma* and *nāmarūpa*. One of the five *tanmātras* or sensible qualities: the color-form that is characteristic of the *tejas* (fire) element.

śabda (m): The sound, verbal testimony, qualified aspect of *Brahman* in its sound OM, one of the five *tanmātras*.

saccidānanda (n/m): Absolute "Existence" (*sat*), "Consciousness" (*cit*) and "Bliss" (*ānanda*). The three consubstantial principles of *Brahman saguṇa*, hence of *ātman*, which are reflected in *jīvātman*.

sādhana (n): Means, appropriate instrument to achieve a certain purpose. Also ascetic discipline (*sādhanā*).

sādhanā (f): Name given to any discipline that is ardently followed with perseverance in order to progress in the spiritual life; ascesis, spiritual effort undergone for realization by the disciple.

saguṇa (adj.): With attributes, qualified; it refers to *Brahman* endowed of *guṇas* (attributes) or the qualified Being, first superimposition on *nirguṇabrahma*. Equivalent to *Īśvara*.

saguṇabrahma (n, m): See *Brahman saguṇa*.

sākṣin (m): Witness, spectator that does not participate and is detached from experiential events and empirical knowledge. It refers to the *ātman* as Witness of the three states.

śakti (f, N): Capability, possibility, potentiality; energy expressing or manifesting power. Virtual power of *māyā*, dynamic energy induced by the presence of the positive immobile pole (*Śiva*); name of the divine Mother as divine primordial energy. Supreme goddess of Tantra.

śama (m): Mental calm; tranquility of the mind that has stopped adhering to the outer and inner objects; cessation of mental projections, extinction of thought movement. One of the qualities, part of the third qualification, of the *Advaita* disciple.

Sāma Veda (m): "Songs of the Veda." One of the four *Vedas*.

samādhāna (n, f): Mental steadfastness. One of the six virtues or qualities, which together constitute the third qualification of the *Advaita* disciple. Condition of continuous concentration on *Brahman*.

samādhi (m): "Contemplation," deep contemplation, transcendent contemplation. Contemplative identity, divine absorption, contemplation in which is attained essential consciential identity. By *nirukti* (traditional etymology), *samādhi* means a consciousness of identity (*sama*) that is transcendent (*adhi*). Constant, uninterrupted and spontaneous influx of consciousness, devoid of fluctuation and distraction.

saṁcitakarman (n): Delayed effect or result of past actions (*karman*) that have accumulated but not reached maturation and actualization in the present state of realization, and which can be easily destroyed.

Sāṁkhya (n): "Enumeration" of twenty-five categories, principles or *tattvas*. Name of one of the oldest *darśanas*. Many of its basic notions have been preserved in other *darśanas*, particularly the distinction between *prakṛti* and *puruṣa*, the conception of *guṇas*, etc. The codifier of this *darśana* was the sage Kapila. In the *Bhagavadgītā*, sometimes the term *sāṁkhya* does not refer directly to the *darśana*, but to upaniṣadic teachings in general, or, more broadly, to analytical, rational teaching.

saṁnyāsa (m): Total renunciation, the last of the four traditional life stages (*āṣrama*). State of consciousness in which the non-reality of the qualifications is recognized.

saṁnyāsin (m): Renouncing ascetic. One who, having comprehended, has renounced everything.

saṁprasāda (m): Constant and imperturbable serenity. *Pax profunda*.

saṁsāra (m): Perennial cycle of becoming; transmigrating within becoming as continual passage through different conditions of consciousness and therefore of existence; indefinite succession of birth-life-rebirth to which liberation (*mokṣa*) puts an end. It corresponds to the uninterrupted chain of cause-effect, for which *karman* ties the individual to becoming.

saṁskāra (m): 1. Preparatory purification rites, for consecration, clothing, etc., preparatory rites in general. 2. Causal "seeds" of action engendered by the tendencies that are present in the mental substance (*citta*) and deriving from experiences, actions, thoughts produced in the present existence as well as in the innumerable prior ones.

saṁyama (m): "Superior discipline." This term indicates the last three steps of Patañjali's *rāja yoga*; they are: *dhāraṇā* or mental concentration, *dhyāna* or meditation, *samādhi* or transcendental contemplation.

Śaṅkara (N): 1. Codifier of *Advaita Vedānta*, the metaphysical *darśana* that transcends religious dualism and ontological monism itself. He lived between 788 and 820 A.D. and compiled important commentaries (*bhāṣya*) to numerous *Upaniṣads*, to the *Brahmasūtra*, *Bhagavadgītā*, and other works, in which he summarizes the teaching and the practice through which to attain *Advaita* realization. He was a disciple of Govindapāda, who in turn was a disciple of Gauḍapāda. He established himself as a strenuous defender of the *sanātanadharma*, the Doctrine of the pure Vedic Tradition, and instituted ten monastic orders to prevent degeneration of spiritual practice. With the codifying of *Advaita* he provided a solid ontological and metaphysical base for all the cults of the time. He founded four monasteries-*maṭhas* at the four cardinal points of India, focal points of the very powerful influence still perceived today.
2. (adj.): "Donating every sort of good," auspicious, propitious, benevolent, giving of joy and prosperity. One of the names of *Śiva* is *Śaṅkara*, he who with his Grace causes *ānanda* at the highest level.

śānta (adj.): Totally pacified, perfectly quiet.

śarīra (n): "Body," "vehicle," shell or sheath (*kośa*); generally three are distinguished: the gross body or *sthūlaśarīra*, subtle body or *liṅgaśarīra* and causal body or *kāraṇaśarīra*.

Śāstra (n): Code, teaching, sacred text. It indicates all sacred Scriptures in general.

sat (n): Being, pure Being. Absolute and pure existence, contrary to *asat*: that which has no existence. *Sat*, *cit*, *ānanda* are the three consubstantial aspects of Being.

sat-cit-ānanda: Absolute Existence (*sat*), Consciousness (*cit*) and Beatitude (*ānanda*). The three consubstantial aspects of *Brahman* and therefore of *ātman*.

sattva (n): Being, existence in itself, essence, wisdom, "intellectual light," one of the three *guṇas* (the other two being *rajas* and *tamas*) that corresponds to equilibrium, harmony, light, purity. In the hierarchical order of manifestation it corresponds to the causal plane, *rajas* to the subtle and *tamas* to the gross plane.

savikalpa (adj.): With differentiation, that which contains in itself differentiation, differentiated, formal.

savikalpa samādhi (m): Transcendental contemplation in which the distinction of subject and object is still latent. It leads to the realization of *Brahman saguṇa*.

Śiva (adj., N, m): Beneficial, propitious, one of the three aspects of the *trimūrti*. The Divine when considered in its transforming and resolving aspect (*mūrti*), but when in union with its *śakti* (*Pārvatī*) it takes the function of creator; as such it is symbolized by the *liṅga*. *Śaivism* separates the aspect of creating from those of conserving and dissolving, so that the aspects that *Śiva* takes and those of the corresponding *śakti* are differentiated, but *Śiva* at the same time is considered as the sole and absolute Principle. For *Vedānta* it is the always and everywhere present One-without-a-second, i.e., *Brahman*.

Śivadharmottara (m): One of the eighteen *upapurāṇas*.

śloka (m): Classic "verse"; consists of four *pādas* of eight syllables. It is the most widespread verse form.

Smṛti (f): Remembered, indirect or "mediated" Tradition.

so 'ham: "I am That." One of the great aphorisms that are found in the *Bṛhadāraṇyaka Upaniṣad*.

sparśa (m): Contact, relation.

śraddhā (f): Faith. Confident adherence to the truth expounded in the Scriptures and by the *guru*. One of the six virtues or qualities, which together constitute the third qualification of the *advaita* disciple.

śrī (N, f): "Prosperity," "luck"; also "holy," blessed: appellation given to the Masters.

Śruti (f): Audition, the Tradition of the "Heard," sacred Knowledge that was "immediately" revealed (*Veda*), what was heard by the ancient Seers (*ṛṣis*) as divine Sounds. One of the names given the *Vedas*.

sthūlaśarīra (n): The gross body, the gross and corporeal forms.

śūdra (m): One of the four traditional social orders (*varṇas*), it is the equivalent of workman. He who lays the foundations of human well-being with service activities.

suṣupti (f): State of deep sleep. Sleep without dream; corresponds to the causal body-plane.

sūtra (n): Thread, rope; aphorism, verse. Text that codifies the fundamental principles of the various philosophical *darśanas*. Metaphorically, the *ātman* that connects all existential planes.

sūtrātma (n): Thread of *ātman* (Self); word that equates to *Hiraṇyagarbha*, subtle universal aspect that comprises the different individualities. "Continuity" of consciousness of *ātman*.

svapna (n): Dream, dream state.

taijasa (adj., m): "Luminous," from *tejas* (fire); the second quarter, *pāda* (foot) of the *ātman*. It constitutes the subtle plane of formal manifest existence and therefore the threefold subtle body (*sūkṣmaśarīra*). It corresponds to *Hiraṇyagarbha* in the universal order.

tamas (n): One of the three *guṇas* (the other two being *rajas* and *sattva*), corresponding to obscurity, inertia, passiveness, to inert immobility, etc. It faces "down," it corresponds to ignorance (*avidyā*), representing the maximum condensation of the potentiality of the being. In the hierarchical order of manifestation it corresponds to the gross plane, *rajas* to the subtle and *sattva* to the causal one.

tanmātra (m): Literally "the measure of this," extension or boundary of something. It indicates the substantial quality of an object, but more specifically of the "elements" that are forming it; also what makes the experience possible through the specific and corresponding sensory organs of knowledge (*jñānendriya*).

tapas (n): Heat, ascetic heat, austerity; ardent aspiration, one of the five *niyamas* of Patañjali's *rāja yoga*.

tarka (m): Philosophical speculation, speculative doctrine, analytical reasoning; also refutation on a logical basis.

tat (pro.): "That." In the *Upaniṣad* it indicates the unqualified Absolute, *Brahman* devoid of attributes or *nirguṇabrahman*.

tattva (n): "Quiddity," truth, principle; category, elemental principle. The twenty-five principles, categories in the *Sāṁkhya darśana*, and the twenty-six in the *Yoga darśana*.

titikṣā (f): Persevering patience coupled with the spiritual ideal. Moral courage. Tolerance garnished by sympathetic understanding. One of the six virtues or qualities, which together constitute the third qualification of the *advaita* disciple.

Turīya (adj., n): The Fourth, "Fourth state" (*caturtha*) which is real and absolute and constitutes the necessary non-dual substratum of all relative states and their contents. *Turīya* is *nirguṇabrahma* and represents the Absolute, Infinite, metaphysical Zero. It can be described only by negations: Non-born, Non-caused, Non-limited, Non-conditioned, Non-determined. It is One-without-a-second (*advaita*) that comprehends and transcends all duality and even the ontological unity itself (*Īśvara*).

tyāga (m): Supreme renunciation, fully effective detachment following discrimination (*viveka*) and recognition of Reality.

upādhi (m): Superimposition, what is superimposed on the Self constituting thereby a "vehicle" and a conditioning at the same time.

Upaniṣad (n): "Sessions or esoteric teaching." Act of "sitting next to someone" in reverential attitude, referring to the disciple at the feet of the Master receiving esoteric knowledge, secret wisdom. For Śaṅkara the purpose of the *Upaniṣads* is to destroy ignorance-*avidyā*, by providing means apt to attain supreme Knowledge.

uparati (f): Inward absorption. One of the six virtues or qualities, which together constitute the third qualification of the *advaita* disciple.

Uttara Mīmāṁsā (f): The second *Mīmāṁsā*, also called *Brahma Mīmāṁsā* or *Śārīraka Mīmāṁsā*, essentially and directly concerns *Brahmavidyā*. Constitutes the *Vedānta*. It is traditionally attributed to Vyāsa.

vāda (m): Doctrine, way, school of thought, path.

vairāgya (n): Detachment from every form of fruit of action, from all conditions and all objects of attachment; renunciation founded on personal reflection and on the teaching from the *guru*.

Vaiśeṣika (n): One of six *darśanas*; Kanāda was the codifier. This *darśana* is directed to the knowledge of individual things as such, considered as distinctive in their own contingent existence.

vaiśvānara (adj., m): "Relative to all human beings," designating the consciousness in the waking state (*jāgrat*). In relation with the individual order, the consciousness state in which the reflection of the *jīva* experiences the exterior empirical or sensorial sphere. Also called *viśva*. In the universal order, it corresponds to the gross-existence sphere constituted of *virāj*. See *Māṇḍūkya Upaniṣad*.

vaiśya (m): The third of the traditional social orders (*varṇas*), that of the producers of wealth.

vaitathya (n): Apparent, illusory.

vānaprastha (m): Hermit, anchorite.

vānaprasthya (n): The third of the traditional stages of life (*āṣrama*). State of he who, having done his duty as head of family, retires into a life of renunciation and meditation. It is a state of consciousness in which the withdrawal from the world is motivated by the *jīva*'s maturity and not by the escape from one's own duties.

varṇa (m): Color, social order. The four traditional social orders: *brāhmaṇa* (sacerdotes), *kṣatriya* (lawmakers or warriors), *vaiśya* (producers of wealth) and *śūdra* (workmen). Also one of the three types of sound (see *śabda*).

vāsanā (f): Subconscious mental impression induced by experience, action and thought, or arising out of indefinite epochs of the past through accumulated *karman*. "Furrows" in the mental substance (*citta*), they constitute the true "seeds" (*saṁskāra*) of thought, and also of rebirth.

Vasudeva (N, m): Patronymic, surname of Kṛṣṇa.

Veda (m): Literally "what has been seen, realized by sages (*ṛṣis*)"; supreme Knowledge, sacred Science. The four great collections: *Ṛg Veda*, *Sāma Veda*, *Yajur Veda* and *Atharva Veda*, contain the exposition of that sacred and traditional Science in its highest expressions and form the *Śruti*.

Vedānta (N, m): "Fulfillment of the *Vedas*." One of the six *darśanas*; also called *Uttara Mīmāṁsā*. The three main streams are: 1) *Vedānta Advaita* (non-dualism), codified by Śaṅkara; 2) *Viśiṣṭādvaita*, also *Dvaitādvaita* or *Bhedābheda* (mitigated or qualified monism), codified by Ramanuja; 3) *Dvaita Vedānta* (dualism), codified by Madhva.

vedānta advaita (m): The non-dualistic *Vedānta* "Point of View" (*darśana*), metaphysical doctrine that transcends dualism (*dvaita*) and monism (*aikya*). Gauḍapāda and Śaṅkara are the founders.

Vedāntasūtra (n): "Aphorisms on *Vedānta*"; another name for the *Brahmasūtra,* Bādarāyaṇa's fundamental work on *Vedānta*.

vicāra (m): Discernment, the faculty of right discerning. Spiritual investigation.

vidyā (f): Knowledge of Reality; consciousness meditation that leads to realization, classified as lower (*apara*) and higher (*para*). The *aparavidyā* is in relation with the first three ends of the human being: *dharma* or rectitude, *artha* or well-being, *kāma* or legitimate desire. The *paravidyā*, expounded in the *Upaniṣads*, regards the ultimate end of the human being: *mokṣa* or liberation.

vijñāna (n): Pure intellect, synonym of *buddhi*, as "synthetic-integrating knowledge" in relation with *manas*. Also Knowledge in the sense of awareness-consciousness.

vijñānamayakośa (m): Sheath made of intellect, envelope of superior intellect, or *buddhi*. Its nature is represented by intellective reason, intuitive discernment. When developed, it balances *manomayakośa*; when made "sattvic" it is able to contemplate universal archetypes.

vikṣepaśakti (f): The projective power of *avidyā-māyā* through which, in place of the Real, it projects the image of the universe of names and forms. It is related to *āvṛtiśakti* (veiling power).

Virāṭ or *Virāj* (adj., m): The totality of the gross manifestation (*vaiśvānara*).

Viṣṇu (N): One of the three aspects of the Hindu *trimūrti*; the Divine, particularly considered under the aspect of the preserver of creation.

Viṣṇu Dharma (m) or *Viṣṇudharmottara* (m): One of the eighteen *Upapurāṇas*.

viśva (n): Represents the totality of gross manifestation; consciousness waking state in the individual order.

vivartavāda (m): "Doctrine of apparent modification."

viveka (m): Intuitive discernment, discrimination between real and non-real, noumenon and phenomenon, which leads to detachment (*vairāgya*) from the non-real and to becoming conscious of Reality.

Vivekacūḍāmaṇi (f): "The Great Jewel of Discernment," title of a work by Śaṅkara that, together with the *Māṇḍūkya Upaniṣad*, is a fundamental text for the realization of *Advaita Vedānta*. In it, a dialogue takes place between a Master and a neophyte wherein all the principal aspects of the doctrine of Non-duality are thoroughly researched in a highly philosophical and poetical way, in both cognitive and operative aspects.

Vyāsa (N): Name of a great *ṛṣi,* considered a manifestation of Nārāyaṇa. According to the Tradition, this name does not indicate an historical or legendary personage, but rather a "intellectual function," a "collective entity" who ordered and permanently settled traditional texts constituting the *Vedas*.

Yājñavalkya (N): One of the great *ṛṣi* of ancient times.

Yajur Veda (m): One of the four *Vedās*.

yama (m): Prohibitions. The first step or means (*aṅgas*) in the *rāja yoga* of Patañjali. The prohibitions are: non-violence, non-appropriation, non-falseness, continence, non-possessiveness.

yoga (m): 1. One of the six *darśanās*, it represents the "doctrine of Union." Not only a philosophy, it proposes operative means to attain "Union." 2. (m): Union, reintegration, complete fusion. Generally the reintegration of the individual into the universal, of the relative (*jīva*) into the absolute (*ātman*).

Yogasūtra (n): Fundamental work in which Patañjali has presented the *sādhanā* of *rāja yoga*, i.e., the appropriate means to achieve "Union" with the *puruṣa*.

yogin (m): One who practices *yoga*, who is advanced in *yoga*, who has attained Union, i.e., is reintegrated into the *ātman*.

RAPHAEL

Unity of Tradition

Having attained a synthesis of Knowledge (with which eclecticism or syncretism are not to be confused), Raphael aims at "presenting" the Universal Tradition in its many Eastern and Western expressions. He has spent a substantial number of years writing and publishing books on spiritual experience, and his works include commentaries on the *Qabbālāh*, Hermeticism and Alchemy. He has also commented on and compared the Orphic Tradition with the works of Plato, Parmenides and Plotinus. Furthermore, Raphael is the author of several books on the pathway of non-duality (*Advaita*), which he has translated from the original Sanskrit, offering commentaries on a number of key Vedantic texts.

With reference to Platonism, Raphael has highlighted the fact that, if we were to draw a parallel between Śaṅkara's *Advaita Vedānta* and a Traditional Western Philosophical Vision, we could refer to the Vision presented by Plato. Drawing such a parallel does not imply a search for reciprocal influences, but rather it points to something of paramount importance: a sole Truth, inherent in the doctrines and teachings of several great thinkers who, although far apart in time and space, have reached similar and in some cases even identical conclusions.

One notices how Raphael writes from a metaphysical perspective in order to manifest and underscore the Unity of Tradition, under the metaphysical perspective. This does not mean that he is in opposition to a dualistic perspective, or to the various religious faiths, or "points of view."

A true embodied metaphysical Vision cannot be opposed to anything.

Written in the light of the Unity of Tradition, Raphael's works, calling on the reader's intuition, present precise points of correspondence between Eastern and Western Teachings. These points of reference are useful for those who want to approach a comparative doctrinal study and to enter the spirit of the Unity of Teaching.

For those who follow either an Eastern or a Western traditional line, these correspondences help us comprehend how the *Philosophia Perennis* (Universal Tradition), which has no history and has not been formulated by human minds as such, "comprehends universal truths that do not belong to any people or any age." It is merely for lack of "comprehension" or of "synthetic vision" that one particular Branch is considered the sole reliable one. Such a position can only lead to opposition and fanaticism. What can degenerate the Doctrine is either a sentimental, fanatical devotion or a condescending intellectualism that is critical and sterile, dogmatic and separative.

In Raphael's words: "For those of us who aim at Realization, our task is to get to the essence of every Doctrine, because we know that just as Truth is one, so Tradition is one, even if, just like Truth, Tradition may be viewed from a plurality of apparently different points of view. We must abandon all disquisitions concerning the phenomenal process of becoming and move onto the plane of Being. In other words: we must have a Philosophy of Being as the foundation of our search and of our realization."[1]

Raphael interprets spiritual practice as a "Path of Fire." Here is what he writes: "...The 'Path of Fire' is the pathway each disciple follows in all branches of Tradition; it is the Way of Return. Therefore, it is not the particular teaching of an individual or a path parallel to the one and only Main Road... After all, every

---

[1] See Raphael, *Tat tvam asi (That thou art):* The Path of Fire according to the *Asparśavāda* (New York: Aurea Vidyā, 2002).

disciple follows his own 'Path of Fire,' no matter which Branch of Tradition he belongs to."

In Raphael's view, what is important is to express through living and being the truth that one has been able to contemplate. Thus, for each being, one's expression of thought and action must be coherent and in agreement with one's own specific *dharma*.

After more than forty years of teaching, both oral and written, Raphael is now dedicating himself only to those people who wish to be "doers" rather than "sayers," according to St. Paul's expression.

Raphael is connected with the *maṭha* founded by *Śrı Ādi* Śaṅkara at Śṛṅgeri and Kāñcıpuram as well as with the Rāmaṇa Āśram at Tiruvannamalai.

Founder of the Āśram Vidyā Order, he now dedicates himself entirely to spiritual practice. He lives in a hermitage connected to the *āśram* and devotes himself completely to a vow of silence.

* * *

May Raphael's Consciousness, expression of Unity of Tradition, guide and illumine along this Opus all those who donate their *mens informalis* (non-formal mind) to the attainment of the highest known Realization.

PUBLICATIONS

Aurea Vidyā Collection

1. Raphael, ***The Threefold Pathway of Fire***: Thoughts that Vibrate for an alchemical, aesthetical metaphysical ascesis.
   ISBN 978-1-931406-00-0

2. Raphael, ***At the Source of Life***: Questions and Answers concerning the Ultimate Reality.
   ISBN 978-1-931406-01-7

3. Raphael, ***Beyond the illusion of the ego***, Synthesis of a Realizative Process.
   ISBN 978-1-931406-03-1

4. Raphael, ***Tat tvam asi*** (That thou art): The Path of Fire According to the Asparśavāda.
   ISBN 978-1-931406-12-3

5. Gauḍapāda, ***Māṇḍūkyakārikā***, The Metaphysical Path of Vedānta.*
   ISBN 978-1-931406-04-8

6. Raphael, ***Orphism and the Initiatory Tradition***
   ISBN 978-1-931406-05-5

7. Śaṅkara, ***Ātmabodha***, Self-knowledge.*
   ISBN 978-1-931406-06-2

8. Raphael, ***Initiation into the Philosophy of Plato***
ISBN 978-1-931406-07-9

9. Śaṅkara, ***Vivekacūḍāmaṇi***: The Crest-jewel of Discernment.*
ISBN 978-1-931406-08-6

10. ***Dṛdṛśyaviveka***: Discernment between *ātman* and non-*ātman*. Attributed to Śaṅkara.*
ISBN 978-1-931406-09-3

11. Parmenides, ***On the Order of Nature*** (Περί φύσεως), For a Philosophical Ascesis.*
ISBN 978-1-931406-10-9

12. Raphael, ***The Science of Love***: From the desire of the senses to the Intellect of Love.
ISBN 978-1-931406-12-3

13. Vyāsa, ***Bhagavadgītā***: The Celestial Song.*
ISBN 978-1-931406-13-0

14. Raphael, ***The Pathway of Fire according to the Qabbālāh*** (Ehjeh 'Ašer 'Ehjeh), I am That I am.
ISBN 978-1-931406-14-7

15. Patañjali, ***The Regal Way to Realization*** (Yogadarśana).*
ISBN 978-1-931406-15-4

16. Raphael, ***Beyond Doubt***: Approaches to Non-duality.
ISBN 978-1-931406-16-1

17. Bādarāyaṇa: ***Brahmasūtra****
ISBN 978-1-931406-17-8

18. Śaṅkara, ***Aparokṣānubhūti***, Self-realization.*
ISBN 978-1-93-140619-2

19. Raphael, ***The Pathway of Non-Duality***
ISBN 978-1-931406-21-5

Related Publications

Raphael, ***Essence and Purpose of Yoga***
The Initiatory Pathways to the Transcendent.
Element Books, Shaftesbury, U.K.
ISBN 978-1-852308-66-7

Śaṅkara, *A brief biography*
Aurea Vidya. New York.
ISBN 978-1-931406-11-6

Forthcoming Publications

Śaṅkara, ***Brief Works,**** Treatises and Hymns.

Five Upaniṣad*, Īśa, Kaivalya, Sarvasāra, Amṛtabindu, Atharvaśira.

Raphael, ***Fire of Ascesis***

Raphael, ***Fire of Awakening***

Raphael, ***Fire of the Philosophers***

* Translation from Sanskrit or Greek and commentary by Raphael

Aurea Vidyā is the Publishing House of the Parmenides Traditional Philosophy Foundation, a Not-for-Profit Organization whose purpose is to make Perennial Philosophy accessible.

The Foundation goes about its purpose in a number of ways: by publishing and distributing Traditional Philosophy texts with Aurea Vidyā, by offering individual and group encounters and by providing a Reading Room and daily Meditations at its Center.

* * *

Those readers who have an interest in Traditional Philosophy are welcome to contact the Foundation at: parmenides.foundation@earthlink.net.

www.ingramcontent.com/pod-product-compliance
Lightning Source LLC
Chambersburg PA
CBHW030232170426
43201CB00006B/196